THE UNITED STATES OF
LAUGHTER

THE UNITED STATES OF
LAUGHTER

One Comedian's Journey Through All 50 States

(an)drew tarvin

ISBN 978-0-9993819-0-8 (Paperback)
ISBN 978-0-9993819-1-5 (eBook)
ISBN 978-0-9993819-2-2 (Audiobook)

Design by Redbrush
Cover by Redbrush

Products from CSz Insights are available at a discount when purchased in bulk or for educational use. For details, contact publishing@cszinsights.com.

CSz Insights
2919 N Halsted St Apt. 3
Chicago, IL 60657
www.cszworldwide.com/books

Printed in the United States of America
First Printing September 2017
10 9 8 7 6 5 4 3 2 1 0 . . . Liftoff!

DEDICATION

To my mom, whose encouragement has made everything I've done possible—and for always laughing at my jokes, even when they aren't very good.

THE JOURNEY

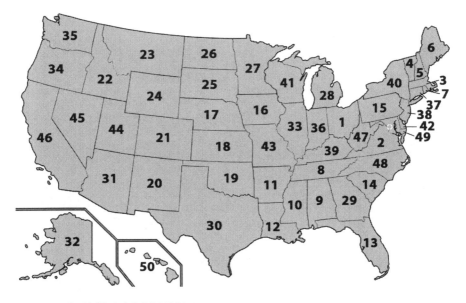

US Map: The Shibboleth / CC-BY-SA-3.0

1. Ohio	18. Kansas	35. Washington
2. Virginia	19. Oklahoma	36. Indiana
3. Massachusetts	20. New Mexico	37. Connecticut
4. Vermont	21. Colorado	38. New Jersey
5. New Hampshire	22. Idaho	39. Kentucky
6. Maine	23. Montana	40. New York
7. Rhode Island	24. Wyoming	41. Wisconsin
8. Tennessee	25. South Dakota	42. Delaware
9. Alabama	26. North Dakota	43. Missouri
10. Mississippi	27. Minnesota	44. Utah
11. Arkansas	28. Michigan	45. Nevada
12. Louisiana	29. Georgia	46. California
13. Florida	30. Texas	47. West Virginia
14. South Carolina	31. Arizona	48. North Carolina
15. Pennsylvania	32. Alaska	49. Maryland
16. Iowa	33. Illinois	50. Hawaii
17. Nebraska	34. Oregon	

PROLOGUE

New York, NY. March 1, 2015

I stood looking at the bare wooden floors of my NYC apartment. The only thing remaining in the place I had called home for the past four years was the dust of a now-empty room and the last few belongings I'd be putting in storage. Outside, snow was starting to fall—a light flurry at first and then harder, like an overeager waiter grinding too much salt on a city of fries.

The snow would continue, racking up inches of accumulation, making my planned drive to Ohio a risky proposition. Rather than meet my doom at the fate of a million tiny frozen water droplets, I decided to wait until the next day to embark on my journey of eighteen months.

New York, NY. March 2, 2015

I stood looking at the bare wooden floors of my NYC apartment. The only thing remaining in the place I had called home for the past four years was the dust of a now-empty room. The last few belongings I was putting in storage were already in the rental van. Outside, there was no snow falling.

As I did one last check of my former home, salsa music played from the restaurant below as workers prepared the grills for the day. The music started every morning at 8 a.m., seven days a week, while I would try to sleep. I'm not a morning person, and the daily unwelcomed blast of melodic rhythms was slowly turning me racist against salsa (the music), salsa (the dance), and salsa (the condiment). It was one of the many reasons I wanted to move out of my second-story walkup in Midtown.

My thoughts turned to my upcoming adventures as a nomad. My first trip wasn't all that exciting: back to Ohio for a few days to crash at my mom's place while I made final preparations for my new location-independent lifestyle.

The reality of the situation started to sink in. As of that moment, I was homeless.

Yes, it was overly dramatic, but what is life without a little exaggeration? People will listen to our "harrowing tales" of sitting in traffic for forty minutes and give their condolences for all that we had to suffer through, so long as it's entertaining.

So I was now homeless. Yes, I still had my most important possessions waiting for me in storage, I had friends and family who were willing to let me crash with them, and I wasn't unemployed. Though I was self-employed, sometimes I think the only difference between unemployment and self-employment is the illusion that we entrepreneurs are doing it on purpose.

But I no longer had a place that was "mine," or even rented at astronomical prices so I could pretend it was mine as long as my rent check cleared each month.

Was I making the right decision? Was it crazy-pants to willingly give up my shelter for permanent travel? Or was it crazier-pants that we ever fully settled down in the first place? Maybe old school hunter-gatherer was the way to go.

The oscillation between "this is a great idea!" and "what have I done?" happened on a near daily (and sometimes hourly) basis since the day I had decided not to renew my lease. In a way, I was confident about the decision. I had no idea what was to come, but I knew in the worst-case scenario it'd at least make for an interesting story. That's the good thing about what I do for a living: any experience, good or bad, can become a story, bit, or learning lesson.[1]

But in another way, I was leaving a great situation for the unknown. I loved living in New York. I loved the energy of the city, the amount of opportunity in so many different fields, and the ability to get pizza at pretty much any hour of the day. I loved walking through the Ramble in Central Park, taking pictures of the skyline from the Brooklyn Bridge, and eating a donut ice cream sandwich at Holey Cream. I loved the efficiency of the city, the pace at which everyone moved, and the fact that people knew to stand on the right side when on an escalator so those of us with things to do can walk on the left.

---

1 Except for maybe what happened in Texas.

And I loved who I had become while living there.

The empty apartment I was standing in was where I went from IT Project Manager at Procter & Gamble to full-time speaker/trainer/comedian. The city I had called home for seven years helped me go from "comedy is a hobby" to "comedy is an integral part of my existence, both mentally and financially."

And, at the ripe old age of thirty-one, I was walking away. Not from my job but the city that birthed it.

My eyes scanned the room one last time as nostalgia seeped from its walls. The two-bedroom, two-living room, half-kitchen, and technically a full bathroom space had hosted several events, including my annual "I'm Still a Kid" birthday party, late-night chats with fellow comedians, and the watching of games (be they football, basketball, or thrones).

I had laughed, cried, and matured there. When I moved to New York in 2008, I was a recent grad with an unclear focus and a nasal voice. By 2015, I had become an established entrepreneur with an empowering passion and a nasal voice.

New York had been home for the past seven years, and I was saying goodbye.

I imagined the scene as if I were in the opening of a movie, where the main character looks at their place one last time and then dramatically turns off the lights before the title comes up on the screen.

I reached out to turn off the lights. Here was the start of my journey, the beginning of a new era of Drew, an adventure unknown to man. Well, specifically, this man—there are plenty of people who have done what I was about to do—but this was a first for Andrew Joseph Tarvin from Cincinnati, Ohio.

I flicked the switch cinematically to start my story, and the lights behind me in the living room went on, so I was now doubly illuminated instead of standing dramatically in the dark—I never could remember which switch turned on which lights in which room.

***

When I started my nomadic journey, I had no idea what to expect, how long it would last, or even why I was doing it. Maybe it was to step outside my comfort zone and begin something new. Maybe it was to challenge myself to see if I could actually pull it off. Maybe I just didn't want to have to go through the asinine process that is finding an apartment in NYC.

In the eighteen months I was without a home, I experienced more than I could have ever imagined. I ate incredible food, went on spectacular adventures, and met fascinating people. And, along the way, I discovered that, despite what we may see on the news or read in the paper, there is one thing that unites all Americans: laughter.

As I traveled around the country, I found connection through comedy. The shared experiences of ridiculous circumstances, everyday situations, and you-had-to-be-there moments helped me realize we are all more alike than we are different, no matter what state we call home. And whether it was a process of discovery or post-crazy-decision justification, this book is the result of me boxing up all my stuff, hitting the road, and seeing the US of A.

The format is simple: each chapter shares a story from that particular state. Some stories are meant to be funny, others a little more poignant. All of the stories are true and accurate, at least to my best recollection, with only slight exaggerations for comedic effect.

The stories are told in the order they happened with connecting points along the way. If you only care about what I said about your state, remember it was just one person's experience. I'm sure everyone has different reactions to different places. Except for Michigan. I'm pretty sure we can all agree that Michigan sucks.

To answer a few common questions:

Are You Crazy?

Not that I'm aware of, though I am an engineer. The idea to become a nomad came about more practically than you might expect.

In 2008, I moved to New York, New York, the world's capital and one of the greatest cities on Earth. It also happens to be the second most expensive city in the United States (just behind San Francisco, way ahead of Des Moines).

At the time of my decision in 2015, I was living in a 600 square-foot apartment, paying double what my friends paid for a three-bedroom house in Ohio. Granted, it's all about location, location, location, and my apartment had an incredible one: 44th and 2nd, right in between Grand Central Station and the United Nations.

What wasn't incredible was its lack of soundproofing and heating. Thin walls meant my ears had the pleasure of hearing constant honking and siren-blaring on 2nd Avenue and a surprising number of protests that took place just below my windows.[2] Terrible insulation and electric heaters meant keeping the apartment at 65°F during the winter led to $400 electric bills.

Combined with the fact that in 2014, I spent more than one hundred

---

2 I'm assuming the protests were because the United Nations Diplomat Center was across the street and not because people thought I was the reason for problems in Darfur.

nights away from home for work (i.e., paying high rent for a place I wasn't in for nearly one-third of the year), the choice to try being a nomad wasn't that far of a leap.

So, I did some research,[3] talked with my friends, and asked myself the three questions I ask when making any major decision:

Question 1: When I lay on my deathbed, what will I regret not having done?

I was confident that, whenever my life should pass before my eyes as I headed for my final snooze, I would regret not having tried a location-independent lifestyle. I already knew what it was like having a home to come back to every day; I'd done it for thirty-one years of my life. The experience of constant travel was something I had only dabbled in during vacations and business trips, and a life on the road seemed enticing. Plus I was at the right life stage to do it (as in not married, no kids, and void of any video games I just had to play).

Question 2: What's the worst that could happen?

I could die. But that's always the answer when you ask that question. The second worst thing was that I might hate it. If that was the case, I could just move back to NYC and pick up where I had left off.

Question 3: What makes for the better story?

Could you tell a story about a pale guy who loves numbers and lives in New York? Yes. In fact, *Sesame Street* did it one-two-three decades ago, ah-ah-ah. But the story of an introverted computer geek turned stand-up comedian becoming a nomad and visiting all fifty states? That's something new, at least for me. Whether the experience led to incredible moments of joy and happiness or induced periods of rage and despair—*spoiler alert:* it did both—that was the better story.

Armed with these answers and incredible support from friends and family, it seemed silly *not* to get rid of most of my possessions, live out of two bags, and head out on the road.

---

3 Chris Guillebeau's work was instrumental in this, and his book, *The $100 Startup*, was the seed that started the whole thing.

What Made It Possible?

The number one thing that made the trip possible was the support from friends, family, and acquaintances I would meet along the way. From people letting me crash on their couch to giving me recommendations of where to go to just being a calm voice in the face of the travel storm, they were instrumental in making the trip feasible and worthwhile.

The second thing was a background in improvisation. Not only were improvisers a large majority of the people listed in the paragraph above, but the "yes, and" mentality also made it easier to deal with the endless rigmarole of travel.[4]

The last thing was my job. I'm a humor engineer. If you've never heard of that, it's because I made it up. I teach individuals, teams, and organizations how to use humor to be more productive, less stressed, and happier. As of writing this sentence, I've helped more than 250 organizations improve employee engagement, increase job satisfaction, and create a more positive workplace culture through comedy, improv, and levity. Why? Because as an engineer, I'm obsessed with efficiency, which is great for computers but not so great for humans. Humans have "emotions" and "feelings," so instead of being efficient, you have to be effective. And one of the best ways to be effective with humans is to use humor.

To accomplish that, I deliver keynote speeches at conferences, facilitate hands-on workshops at company off-sites, and lead full-day training programs with individual teams.[5]

That all involves quite a bit of travel. And when I'm not doing an event, my work can be done from pretty much anywhere that has an internet connection. As a result, engagements for my company, Humor That Works, often dictated (and paid for) where I went. Controlling my schedule and having supreme flexibility were critical to being able to support myself financially throughout the journey.

What Did You Do with Your Stuff?

Prior to the trip, I owned approximately 197 things. I know this because I made a spreadsheet of everything in my apartment.

---

4   It's also led me to accepting my own ideas, like using the word "rigmarole."
5   To learn more about how humor helps you be more effective or to see my programs, visit www.humorthatworks.com.

Here's what I did with it:

- 30 percent was put in storage (59 items)
- 29 percent was given away on Craigslist (57 items)
- 19 percent was thrown out (37 items)
- 16 percent was donated to Goodwill (31 items)
- 6 percent was taken with me in my two carry-on bags (13 items)

For eighteen months, I traveled primarily with just thirteen items, with clothes being one item, encapsulating everything I wore.[6]

Where Did You Go?

I traveled to 142 different cities, all fifty states, fourteen countries, and three continents.[7] I went to some places only once and for just long enough to perform, eat, and see something; others I went to multiple times and stayed for significant durations. But my main focus was on visiting each one of the fifty states.

Why the Fifty States?

I've long had the goal to speak or perform in all fifty states. What can I say? I love completing checklists. Plus it's a cool credit to have:

> Our next speaker has been featured in the *Wall Street Journal*, *Forbes*, and TEDx. He has spoken or performed in all fifty states, lettered in bowling in high school, and is obsessed with milkshakes. Please welcome to the stage, Andrew Tarvin.

Before the start of this journey, I had already done twenty-two states. I figured not having a home was the perfect excuse to try to do even more. When I had done thirty-six states within the first six months of being a nomad, I thought, "Why not shoot for all fifty in a year?" So I did. I went to the states I had never been to and revisited old ones I had yet to perform in, all so that I could say: I visited, spoke, or performed in, took a selfie in, and have a story for all fifty states—and I did it in twelve months.

---

6   To see everything I traveled with, check out tarv.in/packinglist
7   To see a map and calendar of everywhere I went, visit tarv.in/nomadmap

Wait, Didn't You Say You Were a Nomad for Eighteen Months?

I did, and I was. I continued to travel for the six months after I completed my goal of getting to every state in a year. The stories in this book all take place in the first twelve months, between March 1, 2015, and March 1, 2016. Plenty of things happened after the year mark, but my anal-retentiveness won't allow me to stray away from the 365-day window.

What . . . Why . . . How . . . ?

That's enough questions for one prologue. Most of the questions you have are answered in the following pages. If they're not, they're bad questions because I didn't think to answer them.

1. OHIO

The Heart of It All
Mason, OH. March 2, 2015

The sun started to drop below the horizon as we made our way into LaRosa's Pizzeria, a local Cincinnati chain with delicious pizza, amazing breadsticks, and a phone number I'll never forget (347–1111). I was with my mom and, per usual, she was accommodating to my desire for a calzone.

It was the first trip of my nomad journey, and I had come home to Ohio. It would be my third most visited state during my trip (after New York and California), and I would experience countless stories I could tell about my time there. I would go to a fun Buckeye game with Adam, take an epic family trip to the Cincinnati Zoo for the Festival of Lights, and eat tons of Graeters with Matt and Laura. I would speak at some great events, do a ton of hilarious shows, and finally get to play Euchre again.

But none of those trips were more meaningful than my first night back in "The Heart of It All."[8]

Ohio was where I was born and raised, and though it's not the most exciting place to start your travels, I wanted to see my mom before multiple weeks of being out on the road. Some people think that makes me a mama's

---

8   This slogan for Ohio makes sense. It's right about where the heart of the United States would be if it had one, and it's kind of shaped like a heart if you look at it with your eyes half-closed in the dark after staring at the sun for too long.

boy, which I consider a compliment because my mom is awesome.[9] Also, I had to put a few more things into "storage" at her place.

My mom and I sat down in the wooden booth in front of the red-and-white-checkered tablecloth, and I became nostalgic. Not just about the restaurant I had eaten in so many times as a kid, but about time spent just my mom and me.

Growing up, my mom would take me, the youngest of three boys,[10] with her when she would go shopping. It wasn't that exciting, but I always enjoyed it, mostly because she would buy me a Milky Way candy bar at the end of every trip. In the car, we would talk about my day at school, play silly games, and make bad puns off of restaurant names.

"Should we go to Hot Dog Queen for dinner?"

"Nah, how about Black Tent?"

"Hmm, maybe SCs?"

"SCs? I don't get that one."

"Arbys. R. B., S. C."

"Ohhh, no."[11]

It was silly but it made us laugh, something we did a lot of together.

When my parents got divorced, it was my mom and me who lived together as I finished out high school. My oldest brother, Adam, had his own place, and my middle brother, David, was off at college. We survived the tough times by joking our way through the ups and downs as we put everything back together.

Our server came by, and I ordered the same thing I get every time I go to LaRosa's: a four-cheese pepperoni calzone. It's pepperoni and four different kinds of cheese wrapped in a golden-brown triangle of delicious dough that you dip into the perfect marinara sauce.

"Are you excited?" my mom asked.

"For the calzone? Definitely," I replied. "And I suppose for all of the traveling, too. I think it'll be fun, though I'm a little anxious about all the unknowns. Where will I sleep? What if I hate it? How will I watch Buckeye games?" I paused. "How do you feel?"

"About the pineapple pizza I ordered? I feel good about it," my mom said, returning my joke. "You know me, I tend to worry, but I also want you to do whatever makes you happy."

"I know; it's just nerve-wracking not knowing exactly where I'll be in a few weeks, next month, or in a year."

---

9   I believe this sentence confirms that I am, in fact, a mama's boy.

10 Because practice makes perfect.

11 That was Burger King, White Castle, and Arby's for the uninitiated.

"Imagine what it's doing to your dear ol' mother!" my mom said with a smile.

"That's true. You did assume I was kidnapped in Mexico because I didn't respond after a few hours."

"It was more than a few hours. Plus I called David and Woodruff, and instead of them calming me down, they both started getting panicked, too. David called the Mexican embassy, and I started looking at how much money I had in my 401k to see how much ransom I could afford."

"I know, but if you had just called Adam, he would have told you I was flying back that day, and that's why I couldn't respond to your messages. I'm still not sure what you were planning to do."

"Maybe it would've been like that Leslie Nielsen movie where they kidnap his daughter or his wife or somebody."

"You mean *Taken*? Where he says, 'I have a special set of skills'?" I asked.

"Yeah," my mom confirmed.

"That's Liam Neeson. But I like that you were going to take out a bunch of Mexican cartel members."

And that's my mother. Incredibly supportive of us doing what we wanted to do, forever worried about our safety, but willing to do anything for us, and constantly mixing up everyone's names. Leslie Nielsen was in *Taken,* Tom Brokaw played football for the Patriots, and Skittles was that white rapper.[12]

My mom has always been encouraging of the three of us. She was supportive, though cautious, when I moved to New York in 2008, when I left a secure job at P&G in 2012, and when I decided to make this nomadic journey in 2015. Though she was always worried about the risks of my decisions, she was always excited for my new experiences and opportunities.[13]

Our food arrived, and I dug in. I wasn't sure the next time I'd get to enjoy eating comfort food in a comfortable restaurant with someone I was so comfortable with.

During the upcoming eighteen months I was a nomad, my mom would be there for me in so many ways. She would always have a room ready for me when I came to town, she would pick up the snacks she knew I loved, and she would clear her evenings so that we could go to dinner or for a walk. And when I had events in town, she would come to them, even if it meant watching a stand-up set she had already seen fifty-seven times before.

I didn't know any of that was to come, but at that moment, I did know that whatever was on the horizon, I'd be able to get through it because of her.

---

12 Okay, this last one might have been made up; she doesn't even know who Eminem is.

13 We also found a good technological solution to ease her fears: she joined Foursquare so she could see when and where I was checking in. If I was checking into a Wendy's in Savannah, my mom knew I couldn't be dead in a ditch outside of Charleston.

Whatever heart I have in my typically robotic ways comes from her. Whatever compassion I have for helping others is hers. The constant drive for self-improvement, the ability to find joy in everyday moments, and the tendency to sometimes laugh at my own jokes more than others do were all hers.

I could do this. I could be a nomad without going mad because of her support and encouragement.

"This is really good," I said, referring to the calzone but meaning everything about the moment.

"A good meal before you start going everywhere?" she asked.

"The perfect meal before going anywhere," I replied.

We continued to chat and finished our meal. As the waiter dropped off the check, I remembered I had to go to *Microcenter* after dinner to pick up a few more things for my trip.

"Hey, Mom," I said, "I'm going to Macroleft if you want to go with me."

"Sure," she replied with a smile.

Whoever said you can't go home again didn't have a mom like mine.

2. VIRGINIA

Bright Lights
Richmond, VA. March 28, 2015

I stepped out onto center stage, or as we call it, the middle of the playing field. The stage lights shined brightly in my face as the loyal fans eagerly waited to hear what I had to say. I was performing in a ComedySportz match, playing one of my favorite types of games with some of my favorite people.

I was in Richmond, Virginia, for the annual shareholders' meeting for CSz Worldwide, the producers of ComedySportz and an incredible organization comprised of twenty-five CSz cities around the world. Each team is independently owned and operated, but they work together as a collective to bring "for everyone" comedy to fans everywhere.

That "for everyone" mantra is what makes the group so special. More than any other production I've been a part of, ComedySportz is about celebrating the fans who come to see the show, making them the stars of the night as opposed to the performers on stage. The comedy is always appropriate for all ages (think Shrek, not Dora the Explorer) and is one of the funnest types of performance I've ever done.

The annual meeting was where the managers from the individual CSz cities got together to talk about business strategies, city updates, and general tomfoolery. For the past few years, I had been taking an increased role in those meetings, helping to lead the branding committee, and serving on the executive council. This was a bittersweet gathering for me because I was stepping away from a lot of those duties[14] as part of this nomad adventure.

The tradeoff, so far, had been worth it. Since leaving my apartment on March 2, I had been to Ohio and then spent two weeks in Switzerland, Italy, and France. And now I was in Richmond, the Geneva of the South.[15]

But traveling the country out of two bags wasn't without its sacrifices, and stepping away from CSz was one of the biggest ones I was making (that and losing easy access to Shake Shack). CSz had become my tribe, my support network, and my extended family. I was gaining new experiences from my decision but losing my connections to others.

On the playing field, the match continued. Thus far it had been a blast—not a surprise when you're playing with incredibly talented improvisers, many of whom had more than twenty years of improv experience.

The current game I so loved was called Celebrity Punishment, a jump-out style game that involved making puns based off of celebrity names, much like Garth from Wayne's World ("If she were a president, she would be Baber-ham Lincoln").

Like all ComedySportz games, Celebrity Punishment started by getting a suggestion from the audience; for this game, the suggestion was the name of a celebrity.

I was stepping out to make a pun based on Bruce Willis. I took a breath and shared my brilliant joke, "If Bruce Willis was a mediator, he'd be Truce Willis." The audience (mostly) laughed.

I stepped back, while my fellow managers and players stepped in sharing their own jokes on Bruce.

"If Bruce Willis was an amusement park, he'd be Bruce Thrill Us."

"If Bruce Willis was a large smoothie, he'd be Juice Fills Us."

"If Bruce Willis was a pessimist, he'd be Bruce Won'tiss."

ComedySportz was one of my tribes—how could you not love a group who rejoiced in bad puns?

And the members of this tribe were people who had served as my mentors, coaches, confidants, and cheerleaders. I'd learned so much from this fine collection of humans, probably more than any other, in both performance and applied improvisation, and they played a huge role in my transformation from project manager to humor engineer.

When I first joined ComedySportz in 2008, I had just started exploring the use of improv for things other than performance. Then I met people like Patrick and Matt, who took the same improv exercises we used to make people laugh and used them to train corporations on skills like communication,

---

14 Heh, "duties."

15 I'm fairly certain I'm the only person who's ever called it that.

collaboration, and more.

They opened up my eyes to what the intersection of improv and business could look like, laying the foundation for me to start Humor That Works in 2009. The same people making punny jokes about celebrities were the same ones who helped me discover my new career.

I brought my focus back to the match just as the suggestion changed to the surprisingly still popular suggestion of Britney Spears. A few managers shared their lines, and then I stepped out with my brilliance: "If Britney Spears were more advanced, she would be Britney Bow and Arrow."

The audience groaned at the awful joke, which, admittedly, was just as delightful as them laughing.

I tried to appreciate the moment as much as I could, worried that I wouldn't have many opportunities like this coming up. I was no longer at the weekly show in NYC or on the monthly exec calls. I'd probably miss my first CSz Championship in four years. I thought this was goodbye.

Little did I know the people on stage that night would be instrumental in the success of my journey. This show in Richmond wasn't the last I'd be doing with CSz but, rather, the first of twenty that I would do in sixteen cities and thirteen states while being a nomad.[16]

The suggestion changed to JFK. I stepped forward to give what I thought might be my last CSz joke for a while. "If JFK had come a little bit later, he'd be KGL."

A silence hung in the air as the audience processed the terrible attempt at humor. Finally, a wave of laughter spread over the crowd. It was a tiny, relatively quiet wave, but a wave nonetheless.

This was definitely my tribe.

---

16 A huge thank you to the CSz families in Richmond, Boston, Philadelphia, Chicago, Quad Cities, Provo, Minneapolis, New York, Detroit, Los Angeles, Portland, Indianapolis, Sacramento, Milwaukee, Houston, and San Jose.

3. MASSACHUSETTS

Scientifically Justified Road Rage
Outside Boston, MA. May 9, 2015

This is not what I imagined when I signed up to travel indefinitely. I was supposed to be seeing new sights, having new experiences, and eating great food, not sitting in traffic, peeved beyond belief.

The last month had gone swimmingly. After Virginia, I made pit stops in Ohio and New York before heading to Norway, the Netherlands, and Belgium. I arrived back in the States and planned a relaxing road trip through the Northeast. I was taking five days to see five states during the late spring, where the foliage would be blooming and the air would be fresh. Aside from a few shows, I had no obligation but to enjoy myself. And this nimrod in a Toyota Camry was ruining everything.

The morning had started off well: a nice breakfast, a walk in the Arnold Arboretum in Boston, and good conversation with my friend Joe. And then things started going downhill, specifically because they had been barely going at all.

It all started as I was trying to get out of Boston, the worst city for driving in the United States.[17] People think New York is bad, but New Yorkers have an understanding: aggressive driving is the only driving and is to be expected on the crowded city streets.

The Massachusettsan understanding seems to be: none of us are going to

---

17 That's not hyperbole; that's fact according to a report published by Allstate Insurance in 2014.

make up our minds on how to drive, but we are all going to honk about it.

What made matters worse was that the only reason I was currently stuck behind this silver hunk of stupid was that twenty miles back we had passed a "Right Lane Closed Ahead" sign. Immediately people started getting into the left lane, causing slowdowns along the way.

But I've done my research and know that traffic flows much better if you wait until the last moment to merge (not in a jerky way but a "make use of the lanes until you can't" way). I didn't make it up; this is real. They've done the simulations.[18]

So, I attempted to stay in the right lane until the right lane actually ended. Apparently, I was the only one with this knowledge because as we neared the "Right Lane Closed 1 Mile" sign, this inept ignoramus in the Camry decided to be a "hero" and straddle both the left and right lane, preventing me from continuing down my path to righteous efficiency.

I get it. Ill-informed drivers thought I was a jerk because I passed the lane of slow moving cars even though we've all read the same "Lane Closed" signs. But I wasn't a jerk; I didn't think I was more important than everyone else, I just didn't think I should be punished for their ignorance.

Getting mad at people who stay in the lane until they have to merge is like getting mad at people who diet and exercise rather than try the latest miracle health solution. How dare they do something that is scientifically more effective?

So, for a mile, I had to drive at 10 mph in stop-and-go fashion behind a car owned by a stick-figure family of dad, mom, two boys, a dog, and two cats. I only assumed by the way this person drove that the whole family was a disaster, especially the cats.

The best, most infuriating part was that the right lane never ended. The construction sign had accidentally been left up; the right lane was no longer closed, and a jam was created for no reason. Had people stayed in the lane until it ended, we wouldn't have been in that mess to begin with. Or, if "My son is an honor student, but I don't know how to drive" hadn't stopped me from continuing, I would have at least been able to pass those not in the know.

Now the delay meant a long line of semis in the right lane and people going one mile over the speed limit in the left. And that's where I was, stuck behind the Toyota "Let me impose my ignorance on others" Camry for the next fifteen miles.

I tried to relax. I'm generally a pretty calm person. I'm not easily riled and am not prone to emotional outbursts (except when watching the Cincin-

---

18 According to the Coloradoan, the Colorado Department of Transportation says waiting until the last possible moment to merge actually reduces delays by up to 35 percent.

nati Bengals play). It was silly to let something so small affect my mood. I was entering my third month as a nomad, and things had been going according to the loosely connected ideas I called a plan. I was seeing new places, speaking or performing as I went, and capturing stories along the way.

I thought back to the beautiful flowers at the Arboretum. The 280-acre historic landmark was the first public arboretum in North America and was home to more than 14,000 plants. I pictured the pink bloom of the lilacs I had seen on that gorgeous Saturday morning and took deep breaths to calm my nerves.

Every time I was about to reach a place of serenity, Toyota Can't Drive would do something that would upset even the most stoic of monks. The most infuriating were the countless times he could have gotten out of the passing lane and allowed me and anyone else who cared to drive a little faster to get by. But no, in the passing lane he sat, either oblivious to his awfulness or intentional in his fury-building behavior.

I fantasized about being in a James Bond car stocked with missiles because I would have used them to blow this jackbutt off the road. But since I was without artillery, I just vented and shook the steering wheel like it was a hysterical person I was telling to "snap out of it."

You'd think that traveling a lot would make me more understanding of these various travel woes, but it only upset me more. It's one thing to have to sit in traffic on your way home from work; it's another when you have to do it when you still haven't figured out where you're going to sleep that night (or the next night or the next 300, for that matter).

Eventually, after far too long of a time, a small gap opened on the right. I waited a moment to see if poop-for-brains Camry was going to get over, but he didn't. I put on my turn signal, and passive-aggressively shook my head while passing him in the right lane.

I know, you shouldn't pass on the right, but you also shouldn't have to. He was the one that made me tense and forced me to zoom past him. And it was his stupidity that caused me to be in traffic in the first place. That's not my opinion; that's a fact.[19]

---

19 A 2015 report on Vox showed that every state has some type restriction on staying in the left lane and shared a report about how cars sitting in the passing lane can be a huge cause of traffic jams.

What to Call People from Each State

Californian, New Yorker, Massachusettsan. We know what to call people from certain states, but other state identifiers aren't as well known—until now. Here are the demonyms for each state:

Alabama	*Alabaman*	**Montana**	*Montanan*
Alaska	*Alaskan*	**Nebraska**	*Nebraskan*
Arizona	*Arizonan*	**Nevada**	*Nevadadada*
Arkansas	*Arkansasian*	**New Hampshire**	*New Hampshirean*
California	*Californian*	**New Jersey**	*New Jersene*
Colorado	*Coloradan*	**New Mexico**	*Nuevo Mexicano*
Connecticut	*Connecticutter*	**New York**	*New Yorker*
Delaware	*Delawarewolf*	**North Carolina**	*North Carolinan*
Florida	*Floridian*	**North Dakota**	*North Dakotan*
Georgia	*Georgian*	**Ohio**	*Ohiobo*
Hawaii	*Hawaiian*	**Oklahoma**	*Oklahombre*
Idaho	*Idahomer*	**Oregon**	*Oregano*
Illinois	*Illinoisemaker*	**Pennsylvania**	*Pennsylvaner*
Indiana	*Indianan*	**Rhode Island**	*Rhode Islandier*
Iowa	*Iowaldo*	**South Carolina**	*South Carolinan*
Kansas	*Kansian*	**South Dakota**	*South Dakotan*
Kentucky	*Kentucker*	**Tennessee**	*Tennesseen*
Louisiana	*Louisianananan*	**Texas**	*Texan*
Maine	*Mainestay*	**Utah**	*Utern*
Maryland	*Marylando*	**Vermont**	*Vermontaineer*
Massachusetts	*Massachusettsan*	**Virginia**	*Virginian*
Michigan	*Michigander*	**Washington**	*Washingtoner*
Minnesota	*Minne-so-tan*	**West Virginia**	*West Virginian*
Mississippi	*Mississipper*	**Wisconsin**	*Wisconsinite*
Missouri	*Missourito*	**Wyoming**	*Wyominger*

NOTE: These are 100 percent factually correct.[20]

---

20 These are not 100 percent factually correct.

4. VERMONT

What Brings You to Vermont?
Montpelier, VT. May 9, 2015

"I enjoyed your little comedy skit," an old man's voice said over my shoulder, startling me and causing the water in my mouth to spurt between my lips.

It was Saturday night, and I had just finished a spot on a stand-up show in the second state of my Northeast tour. I was watching the rest of the show when I was surprised into conversation. I swallowed the remaining water in my mouth, set my bottle down, and turned toward the voice.

It had come from a man who looked to be in his mid-fifties, far younger than his voice would suggest. He stooped over, shorter than me, though I imagined if he had any semblance of posture he'd be nearly six feet tall. He had short black hair and a weathered face. He was missing two of his front teeth, and you could see his tongue sitting in his mouth when he smiled.

What I wanted to say was, "When you see someone do stand-up or improv comedy, it's called a 'set.' If they're acting out scenes, it's called a 'sketch.' Or you could say 'show' for any of them, but never 'little comedy skit.' It's not an elementary school talent show."

What I did say was, "Thank you."

"What brings you to Vermont?" he asked, his tongue flopping around like a dying fish. My worst fears were confirmed: he wanted to talk.

As an introvert, small talk is one of the most draining activities on the planet, just behind running an ultra-marathon while taking the SATs, and it was something I usually tried to avoid.[21]

Conversation with strangers was one of the prices I had to pay for a location-independent lifestyle—it's hard to retreat to your room when you don't, in fact, have a room. But, according to Dale Carnegie, the key to being a good conversationalist is to get the other person to start talking and then shut up; it's how you win friends *and* influence people. So I tried out a conversation deferment tactic to shift focus back on the old man by repeating his question to him.

"I'm traveling to all of the states," I replied, "What brings you to Vermont?"

"Me?" the old man who we'll call Roland answered.[22] "I've been here my entire life. In fact, I've been coming to this here bar for thirty-five years."

Conversation deferment successfully deployed.

"This here bar" was the self-proclaimed world-famous Charlie O's in Montpelier, Vermont. And it was very much a bar. It had slightly tilted pool tables that served just as much as beer holders as a place to actually play pool; the walls were filled with kitsch from garage sales from across the country, and it was patronized by an eclectic clientele ranging from young twenty-somethings to the Roland generation.

From both the inside and out, it had the feel of a Wild West saloon updated to the '70s. The sign out front offered, "Good drinks and bad company since the war between the states."

"Wow, thirty-five years? You must really like this bar." I replied.

"I do," he answered. "Want to know why?"

"I do," I said because I did want to know why. Any place that has a thirty-five-year retention rate is surely doing something right. Plus, the more he talked, the less I had to.

"Well, thirty-five years ago, around this same time of year, I came in for the first time. In fact, I was standing right over there." He pointed emphatically to the end of the bar near the door. "Now, I will admit, I had had a few drinks. Maybe three, maybe ten, who knows. Anyway, I was at the bar ordering another drink when I accidentally bumped the man next to me."

Roland bumped into me to demonstrate what he meant (even though I already knew what he meant).

"Well, the man was not happy about that, so he pulled out his gun."

---

21 Growing up, I took the advice "Don't talk to strangers" to heart, not out of fear of being kidnapped but out of dread of having to talk to another person.

22 I'm just assuming that was his name. I never actually asked him what it was, but, according to BabyNamester.com, Roland was more popular as a boy's name in Vermont than in any other state in 1960, so it seems almost guaranteed that's what he was called.

Surprised at the immediate escalation of the story, I nearly shouted "He pulled out his gun?!?[23]"

"He pulled out his gun," he repeated. "Now I'm no stranger to guns. We love 'em here. But I'll be damned if I wasn't scared. I went from ordering a beer to having a pistol in my face."

Roland paused, his tongue sitting there.

"But you know why I love this bar?"

I had no idea. I didn't think getting a gun pulled on you was a sign of "Hey, you should keep coming back here." So, I asked why.

Roland smiled. "Because without missing a beat, the bartender pulled out a shotgun, pointed it at the man with the gun, and yelled 'Out!' And the man with the gun looked at the bartender. Then he looked at me. Then he looked at the bartender. Then he looked at me. Then he looked at the bartender. Then he looked at me . . ."

(He was really drawing out this part of the story.)

". . . looked at the bartender, then at me. Then he chugged his beer, slammed the glass on the counter, and left."

"And that's why you've been coming to this here bar for thirty-five years?" I confirmed.

"Yup. Any place that has a shotgun behind the counter and ain't afraid to use it is fine by me. That's why this is my second favorite bar in Vermont."

And with that, our conversation trailed off. Roland headed back to the gun spot to order another drink, and I headed back to my hotel. I was happy I had stuck around. I had almost left immediately after performing, but the cost of small talk had definitely been worth it to hear Roland's story.

It wasn't until about an hour later that I got struck with a deep curiosity: if Charlie O's was his second favorite bar, what happened at his favorite bar?[24]

---

23 I couldn't write this sentence without thinking of R Kelly's *Trapped in the Closet*.

24 I'm going to assume his first favorite bar was somehow related to how he lost his two front teeth, maybe in a knife fight with someone else he had bumped into.

5. NEW HAMPSHIRE

Chasing Waterfalls
White Mountain National Forest, NH. May 10, 2015

I drove east on US-302, rocking out to Adele's *21* as the trees of White Mountain National Forest blurred past on either side. In the distance, the peaks of Mt. Washington and Mt. Adams continued defrosting, no longer the white tops from whence the park got its name.

I was traveling through New Hampshire on my way from Vermont to Maine and had taken a detour through the mountains in hopes of getting a good picture to commemorate the state of those who would "Live Free or Die."[25]

As I made my way through the forest (and the chorus of "Set Fire to the Rain"), I saw an opening on my left and in it, a waterfall. I slowed down and pulled into a parking area on the right. Adele's aching heart would have to wait, as I had found my photo.

There's something captivating about waterfalls. Maybe it's the mesmerizing flow of water succumbing to gravity and crashing to the Earth. Or maybe it's just nature's way of balancing the wonder that comes from staring at a fire or standing in a breeze (throw in the beauty of mountains and a little bit of heart, and you end up with Captain Planet).

Whatever it is, it makes waterfalls my favorite type of body of water. No, TLC, I'm not going to stick to the rivers and the lakes that I'm used to be-

---

25 I'm not talking about John McClane.

cause they are nothing compared to the beauty of water dropping over a steep cliff in the middle of nature.

So of course I needed a picture. I crossed the street and made my way to the base of the falls. The main fallage took place on the left, a powerful flow of water spewing onto rocks above before making a thirty-foot drop into a shallow pool. To the right, a smaller waterslip streamed down a stair of stone before dribbling into a poodle-sized puddle. I climbed the middle to get a better view.

I made it halfway up the cliff before getting stuck with no real place to go, so I turned around and admired the surroundings. I could feel the mist of the falls leaving tiny droplets of water on the ends of my arm hair, like a disgusting hair-plus-water lollipop for ants.

I took a seat and a moment to enjoy the sights and sounds of my loca-tion. Just the day before, I had been infuriated on my drive up from Boston, and now I was at peace in nature, away from traffic, construction, and stupid Toyota Camrys.

Ahead of me lay the forest of trees I had passed, the spring air preview-ing the warmer weather to come. The sound of falling water was soothing (as opposed to the sound of dripping water, which is insanity inducing), and I got lost in thought.

I thought about how thankful I was for gravity for creating such a beautiful setting (and for keeping us from spiraling through space). I thought about how gravity is this invisible force that binds the world together in mysterious unknown ways, kind of like Gorilla Glue. I thought about *Gravity*, the movie, and how it probably should have just been a short film. I thought about Sandra Bullock, and how I'll always associate her with the movie *Speed*, though her co-star Keanu, will always be associated with *The Matrix*. I thought about, how in *The Matrix*, gravity didn't apply to Neo.

I thought about how there was all this water flowing freely right next to me, and yet in California, they were amid a massive drought, and how, with global warming, that drought would get worse, but other places would get more not-drought. I thought about rising sea levels and how New York City would become a modern-day Atlantis. I thought about how, to all the people who consider the Midwest "flyover country," living there would start looking pretty good if NYC was underwater and LA was on fire. I thought about how I was the only one who could prevent forest fires. I thought about how if there were a fire, they would probably need this free-flowing water next to me.

I thought about the thoughts that I was thinking. I thought about how weird it was that we humans think and wondered how other animals' thinking compared to our thinking, and whether they ever thought about what we were thinking. The thought of them thinking about our thoughts made me think. It also made my brain hurt.

After what felt like two hours but was more likely two minutes, I finished my thoughts and headed down the falls to continue my drive. I enjoyed moments of contemplation but also had things to do. Life as a nomad wasn't just one long vacation; I still had to work, still had to get things done, and still had to not spend all day sitting on a waterfall.

As I was coming down, a bus pulled into the parking area and a dorm of college students ascended upon the falls. I stopped to take a quick selfie before any of them could ruin my perfect backdrop, and as I put my camera down, one of the students asked if I wanted them to take my picture.

My thoughts were still flowing like the water around me, and I thought about how years ago, before the days of self-facing cell phone cameras, I absolutely would have wanted my picture taken, and as a result, I probably would have had a more in-depth conversation with this fellow human. They would take a picture on my digital camera that I would review, and I would ask for one or two more based on what I saw.

A few years before digital cameras became mainstream, they would have taken a picture, and I would have to wait to see what the picture looked like after I got the film developed, either cursing or rejoicing as I flipped through the photos in a Walgreens.

And before that, I would have had no picture at all. All I would have were the descriptions of what I saw or perhaps, what I thought I saw.

And then I thought about how none of that mattered because we were in the age of selfies and self-sufficiency, so I said no and left. After all, there were more miles to be driven, more work to be done, and more Adele to be sung.

6. MAINE

The Sea's All That
Cape Elizabeth, ME. May 11, 2015

I sprinted through the wooded path, my breath growing heavier with each step. I was in pretty good shape, but the intervals of starts and stops were reminding me that I wasn't as spry as I used to be.[26]

The density of the woods began to dissipate, and I ran through an opening in the trees where I was immediately stopped in my tracks. A short burst of wind had struck my whole body, startling and awakening me at the same time.

At that moment, I realized I should stop. I should stop running. Not because my workout was too exhausting but because I wasn't even working out in the first place.

I was in Two Lights State Park in Maine, and I was simply trying to see the park as efficiently as I could. I ran from landmark to landmark, stopping to take a quick picture and then moving on. And I don't mean figuratively running as in being in a bit of a hurry. I mean running as if I were in a race to get from the fire tower to the playground to the observation point as fast as my legs would take me.

It was a result of my obsession with efficiency. I've been obsessed with doing things as quickly as possible for as long as I can remember. Or really, since before I can remember because I was born three weeks early. Apparently,

---

26 As evidenced by the fact I just used the word *spry*.

even in the womb, I was like "I don't need a full nine months; I'm ready to go right now. Let's do this, Mom. I've got things to do!"

That obsession carries over into almost everything in life. I once spent an entire day figuring out the most efficient allocation of pocket real estate. There were diagrams, timed run-throughs, and more than a few moments of contemplating whether I should just buy a fanny pack.[27]

At the moment, efficiency was dictating my travels. When I started my adventure, I told myself I needed to visit at least one place in every state, partly so I could honestly say I saw the United States, but more so because I assumed it would make for a better story. I was now in the fourth state of my Northeastern road trip and had turned my "stop and smell the roses" moments into "slow down and get a light whiff of whatever you can." I moved quickly from spot to spot because I didn't want to miss a thing, but I also didn't want to take too much time to do it.

I realized I wasn't going to these places for the joy of seeing them but for checking off some imaginary list in my head. When I have a checklist, I want to get through it as fast as I can, even if that checklist includes "see nature and enjoy yourself." I think, *okay, enjoyed myself for five minutes, what's the next task? Meditate? Okay, how do I meditate as quickly as possible?*

What made the drive for efficiency even more tempting was that I had good reason for being quick: I was on a tight schedule. I wanted to see some nature, but I also had a show later that night, and I wanted to go back to my hotel room beforehand, and I knew I should probably eat something, and I needed to send out few emails *and, and, and.*

But the wind made me stop. It wasn't that the wind was too strong—though at 140 pounds, I will admit I have lost to the wind in the past. But it served as a smack in the face to slow down, take a moment to appreciate my environment, and see what was in front of me. It was the Atlantic Ocean.

I took a few breaths of the Atlantic air as the sun lingered in the afternoon sky. Rocks that looked like petrified wood jutted from the earth in front of me. As I walked out onto them, I had a feeling that this moment was somehow momentous.

Not necessarily because it actually was momentous but because I had mentally made it so. It was as if I were in a movie, and I just realized I should stop my ex from getting on that plane, or I should patch things up with my best friend who was just trying to help, or maybe Captain America was right after all.

The wind remained a steady constant, like a giant industrial fan they use

---

27 In the end, fashion said no fanny pack, so I went with phone in the left pocket, keys, and wallet in the right.

to make a model's hair flow, and I stood there, taking in the view, having my movie moment.

It was a classic tale, the protagonist being so busy they didn't see the beauty that was around them. Here I was on a Monday afternoon, looking out at the Atlantic Ocean, as part of a larger journey, and I had barely noticed it. I was Freddie Prinze Jr., and nature was Rachael Leigh Cook.

I was so close to missing it entirely. In an attempt at being efficient, I had almost skipped the dirt trail that led me to this view. I wondered how many things in life I've missed in an attempt to get to where I was going instead of enjoying the journey along the way.

I often talk about the difference between efficiency and effectiveness in my training programs, that we've become so obsessed with being efficient that we don't always stop to see if we're actually effective. But I don't always practice what I speech.

It's perfectly fine to want to do a lot of things efficiently; there's no sense in leisurely doing dishes or not walking up an escalator. But if we save time, we should also be willing to spend it. Because the reality is that the time will pass anyway, and we might as well take time to enjoy it.

I reached down to touch the ocean as the waves crashed on a nearby rock. The water was cold and a little icky, and I regretted it pretty much immediately. But technically I had now been in the Atlantic Ocean, even if the only part that had been in was the fingernail of my middle finger on my left hand.

I took another moment to enjoy the coastal setting, impressed that I had somehow turned a run through the park into an opportunity to cast myself as Freddie Prinze, Jr.

These were the moments worth pausing for—moments when you can take a break from the day, enjoy a park with an ocean view, and come up with an elaborate metaphor about a '90s romcom just to end it with a terrible pun: Sea's All That.

Where to Stop and Smell the Roses in Each State

I was successful in visiting at least one place in every state. So, if you find yourself in a new place and you're looking for somewhere to relax for a bit, here's where to go.

State	Place	State	Place
Alabama	*Space & Rocket Museum*	**Montana**	*Montana State Capitol*
Alaska	*Mendenhall Glacier*	**Nebraska**	*Heartland of America*
Arizona	*Grand Canyon*	**Nevada**	*Hoover Dam*
Arkansas	*The Big Dam Bridge*	**New Hampshire**	*White Mountains Forest*
California	*Kelso Dunes*	**New Jersey**	*Hoboken Waterfront*
Colorado	*Pikes Peak*	**New Mexico**	*Kasha Katuwe*
Connecticut	*Guiffrida Park*	**New York**	*Central Park*
Delaware	*Center for Creative Arts*	**North Carolina**	*Duke Uni*
Florida	*Johnson Beach*	**North Dakota**	*North Dakota State Uni*
Georgia	*River Street*	**Ohio**	*Mt. Adams*
Hawaii	*Aloha Tower*	**Oklahoma**	*Myriad Gardens*
Idaho	*Craters of the Moon*	**Oregon**	*Coe Circle Park*
Illinois	*Casey, IL*	**Pennsylvania**	*Thousand Steps Hike*
Indiana	*White River State Park*	**Rhode Island**	*Cliff Walk*
Iowa	*Iowa State Capitol*	**South Carolina**	*South of the Border*
Kansas	*Underground Salt Mine*	**South Dakota**	*Badlands Natl Park*
Kentucky	*Devou Park*	**Tennessee**	*Centennial Park*
Louisiana	*Louisiana State Uni*	**Texas**	*The Alamo*
Maine	*Two Lights State Park*	**Utah**	*Arches Natl Park*
Maryland	*Inner Harbor*	**Vermont**	*Quechee Gorge*
Massachusetts	*Arnold Arboretum*	**Virginia**	*Maymont*
Michigan	*Belle Isle*	**Washington**	*Kerry Park*
Minnesota	*Minnehaha Park*	**West Virginia**	*Tamarack*
Mississippi	*Vicksburg Military Park*	**Wisconsin**	*Milwaukee Market*
Missouri	*Tower Grove Park*	**Wyoming**	*Yellowstone*

7. RHODE ISLAND

The No Corner Office
Newport, RI. May 12, 2015

I looked away from my screen to think, hoping the environment around me would provide more inspiration than staring at black text on a white background.

Before my nomad journey started, looking away from my computer often meant seeing my roommate Pat sitting at his desk in our home office. Before leaving P&G, looking away meant seeing coworkers gophering up and down in the rows of cubicles. Before moving to NYC, it meant seeing nothing but barren walls and offices for the titled.[28] Right now, it meant seeing the Atlantic Ocean.

I was sitting on a bench along the Cliff Walk in Newport, Rhode Island. I had time before my show that night and needed a place to work. I had thought about going to a Starbucks or local coffee shop but saw the ocean first and figured I would get one last view of it before my Northeast road trip concluded.

Working out in nature has its disadvantages. There are no power outlets for keeping your computer alive or recharging your phone. There are

---

28 My first job out of college was in a building that housed R&D and engineering at P&G. Much of the work that took place there was proprietary and wouldn't be seen by the public for five-plus years. Consequentially, the only "window" in the building was a webcam an engineer had set up that showed the outside world. If you wanted to see what the weather was like or get a view of outside, you just brought up your browser and went to a specific IP address. In that way, we all had an office with a view.

no restrooms for resting and no sinks for splashing water on your face when you're stressed out and want to pretend you're in an action movie. There are no baristas mispronouncing your name or pots of terrible coffee. There are no meeting, conference, or huddle rooms. There are no rooms at all.

Instead, there is nature. There is the sun, clouds, birds, bees, and, in my case that day, waves crashing against the shore. Some people have the ocean as their desktop background; I had it as my IRL background.

To my left, a few seagulls did whatever it is seagulls do; further down surfers in wetsuits were preparing to ride the three-foot waves. To my right, down a paved path that clung to the ridge above the water, you could see mansions lining the coast, each one bigger than the last. Directly before me, clouds in the shape of ink stains and Rorschach tests dotted the sky. Below that, you could see the sun ripple off the water. Below that was the glow of my computer screen.

The cursor blinked at me, taunting my writer's block. I was working on some stand-up, and the furthest I had gotten was writing out the abbreviations for each of the fifty states. When I was in Maine, I had noticed how they liked to use their state abbreviation, ME, in marketing campaigns: Bike ME, I Love ME, Don't Ever Leave ME.

The premise for the joke I was trying to figure out was how other states could do similar things with their abbreviations. What could Ohio do with OH or Georgia with GA? I let my mind wander as I stared out at the ocean:

- OH no? OH, yes!
- You'll go GAGA for Georgia.
- Come to Omaha N-E time you want.

A disruption from the nearby seagulls brought me back from my paltry comedic brainstorm. If I had to guess, the gulls were either upset over the current income disparity in the country or over a piece of granola bar a passerby had just dropped.

I guess that was one advantage of a traditional workspace: office workers don't typically have to deal with noisy seagulls. Sure, they have to contend with interrupting coworkers, constant meetings, and a bland work environment, but no one fights over scraps of food.[29] But since starting my own business, I realized there were advantages to having an office to go to every day.

First, there's the mental shift of "going" to work. You can mentally prepare during your morning commute and, more importantly, mentally de-stress when you leave work. When your workplace is your play place, eat place, and

---

29 Except for when they are donuts in the break room. Then we all act like seagulls.

sleep place, the line between work and life becomes blurred. You never physically leave work, which sometimes means you never mentally leave it, either.

Second, a workplace unites you with coworkers. Depending on who you work with, that might seem like a gigantic negative, but it can mean connection, collaboration, and commiseration. Even for an introvert, having people to bounce ideas off of, check in with, or even just talk to is a major component of being a functioning human being.

My business was a company of one; it was one of the greatest pros and biggest cons of working for myself. But before I left NYC, I at least had Pat.

Pat and I worked really well together as roommates and office coworkers. We had set up one of the rooms as our workspace so that we could mentally go to work (and write off a bigger portion of our rent for tax purposes). And we could go an entire day without saying a word to each other. We didn't feel it necessary to engage in small talk just because we passed each other in the living room, and we never felt like the other person was mad at us because we were quiet. We were content to focus on what we needed to get done.

But, when either of us wanted or needed to talk something out, we were there for each other. I could bounce joke ideas off of him; he could get my thoughts on a client he was working with. When he sneezed, I would sympathetically tell him to shut up.

As a nomad, I had no coworkers, no co-creators, and no Pat. Over the last five days, the only people I had talked with were the hosts of the shows I was performing on, a few people in Boston, and Roland.

For the first time in the last two months, I felt lonely. I, a proud introvert,[30] wanted someone to talk to. Well, not just anyone, I still didn't want to have to talk to strangers, but I wanted to talk with a friend. I felt alone and didn't like the feeling.

Actually, I didn't like any feelings that weren't completely positive. It was my concession to being a human: embrace emotions but only the positive ones. So I did what I always do when a negative emotion crops up, I ignored it and got back to work.

I stared at my computer because that's where the work was and the emotions weren't. There was a lesson to be learned in that moment, but I wouldn't learn it until later.

Instead, I focused on the state abbreviations. I needed a new angle to the joke. Maybe instead of using abbreviations themselves, the humor was in using full state names when you would normally use the sound from the abbreviation:

---

30 Specifically, I'm a Blue Square, Conscientious INTJ with the sign of Aquarius.

- "Say Hawaii to your mom when you see her."
- "Missouri Money, Missouri Problems."
- "Do Re Michigan Fa So Louisiana Ti Do."

A jogger hustled by on the path. I considered stopping her to ask what she thought about my work, something I would've done with Pat. But I realized if she was running it meant she was probably late for a meeting, and there was no way she was as funny as my old roommate.

I was on my own. I read through the jokes I had written. They weren't hilarious, I decided, but they were Oklahoma.

8. TENNESSEE

Coming a Long Way
Nashville, TN. May 17, 2015

A light drizzle fell as I ballerina'd down a puddle-soaked sidewalk, headed toward The East Room. I was in Nashville, Tennessee, the first stop on a brand-new road trip, this one through a few southern states. After leaving Providence (the city in Rhode Island, not the protective care of a spiritual being), I took a short break in New York before hitting the road again to check off eight states over two weeks and 4,000 miles.

I opened the door to the venue and stepped inside. Seated at a table near the front was a pleasant young lady playing with a small furry creature.

"Hi, I'm here for the stand-up show," I said, interrupting her playtime.

She looked up from her pet and smiled. "Welcome. Technically we're not opening the house for ten more minutes, but you can come in out of the rain."

"Thank you," I replied. "I'm one of the comedians on the show. Is that a mouse you have there?"

"Oh, in that case, double welcome! Let me get Chad," she replied calmly before yelling, "Chad!" A bearded man with an oval face and rectangular glasses started to make his way over as the lady continued, "It's actually a flying squirrel, so like a mouse with wings."

Before I could process her last statement, Chad introduced himself.

"Hey Chad," I replied, "I'm Drew Tarvin. We chatted briefly via Facebook. Thanks for having me on the show."

"No problem, we're happy to have you. So you know Laura?" he asked.

"I do," I answered. "We went to school together."

There was a moment of awkward silence, so I tried to break the ice. "Did you know she has a flying squirrel?" I said, nodding toward the flying squirrel whisperer.

"I did. This is my girlfriend, Mary. We both have flying squirrels."

That's when I noticed the little creature sitting in Chad's breast pocket. So they did. Two out of the two people I had met so far in Nashville had pet flying squirrels. With that small sample size, it seemed safe to assume that 100 percent of the citizens of Nashville owned winged rodents.

"Hello, Drew Tarvin," said a woman's voice from the performance space.

I looked over in time to see Laura coming in for a hug.

"Oh my God, it's been so long," she said as we exited our embrace.

She was right; it had been a long time, nearly ten years. We met while we were both earning our degrees from The Ohio State University. Mine was in computer science and engineering; hers was in visual communication design. We were both now professional comedians.

This transition, engineer to comedian, surprises a lot of people. I recently went to my high school reunion, and when old classmates found out I did comedy, they said, "But you're not funny." Growing up, I was never the life of the party or the class clown; I was an introverted computer geek who was voted teacher's pet.

But while I was at Ohio State, my best friend wanted to start an improv group; he needed people and forced me to join. Together, we co-founded The 8th Floor Improv Comedy Group with a few friends, and we were terrible. We had no idea what we were going; we just watched *Whose Line Is It Anyway?* and tried to repeat what we saw. But over time, with practice, repetition, and a lot of bad shows, we got better. And a year after forming the group, I did my first stand-up comedy show.

The show was a stand-up competition, the quarter-finals of a yearlong contest that would culminate in finals in the spring. Also performing that night were twelve other amateur comedians, including a few fellow 8th Floor members and this woman named Laura Sanders.

And nine years, five months, and three days after that show, on a stage in Nashville, Tennessee, Laura and I were once again reconnected.

"I know!" I said. "I don't think I've seen you since college. How are you?"

"I'm good," Laura replied. "How are you?"

"I'm good."

Master of small talk I am not. What do you say to someone you barely knew in college that you're now seeing for the first time in ten years?

"Thanks for having me on the show," I finally said.

"Of course, it was great that you reached out," she replied. "What a small world."

What a small world indeed. Coincidence (and Facebook) had brought Laura and me back to share the same stage after all these years. I had been looking for a spot I could perform while in Nashville when I came across The East Room, a music venue and bar that also hosted a comedy show on off nights. The comedian headlining the day I was going to be in town was none other than Laura Sanders, fellow Ohio State Buckeye and former stand-up competition rival. I reached out on Facebook, and she got me a guest spot on the show.

Laura and I chitchatted a while longer before prepping for the upcoming performance. Shortly after 18:30, Chad took the stage and kicked off the night.

As he warmed up the crowd, I realized the venue was perfect for concerts. Comedy? Not so much. The stage was three feet high, and the space immediately in front of it was reserved for dancing and moshing, two activities that don't typically happen during stand-up. The high ceilings were ideal for air circulation but terrible for creating an intimate space where laughter could reverberate. From the stage, you had to look down at the audience, which made me feel a bit like a Greek god bestowing one-liner commandments to all the believers below.

Chad's set was followed by a few local comedians, and then it was me. I did a respectable ten minutes before making way for the main event. First was Justin Golak, a co-producer of Laura's Second Shift Comedy Tour, and then it was Laura to close out the night. She crushed it.

We both had come a long way since our first show together so many years ago. Laura was now sporting a much shorter haircut and had an incredible stage presence that did justice to her well-written material. I had finally started wearing clothes that fit, and I had come to feel at home on stage with a microphone. My material had also changed. My first set back at Ohio State included clichéd jokes, obvious punchlines, and a not-so-subtle male anatomy joke. Eventually, I had come to embrace my engineering point of view and had decided long ago not to go blue.[31]

Laura and I caught up after the show, talking about what we were currently up to and reminiscing about days gone by. We traded "war stories"

---

31 "Going blue" in comedy means cursing and/or talking about sex, drugs, and rock 'n' roll. My material is now rated Mom, as in I always want my mom to be comfortable watching my shows. (Told you I was a mama's boy.)

of our stand-up careers, talked about our lives outside of comedy, and remembered back to Amateur Comedy Night at OSU.

"Do you remember your first stand-up set?" I asked Laura.

"Of course," she replied, "you never forget it. It was fall quarter, and the show was at Woody's in the old Union. I was so nervous."

"I know; I couldn't eat the entire day. Though that was nothing compared to the semi-finals winter quarter. I don't know if you remember, but I completely blanked on stage that night."

Yep. It was one of my worst experiences as a comedian. It was the semi-final round of the competition in front 200-plus people. Daniel Tosh, Mark Curry, and Jo Koy sat at a table on stage while each comic performed and then rated them afterward. It was the fourth stand-up show I had ever done.

Three minutes into my set, I completely forgot what I was going to say. I had memorized everything word for word and suddenly drew a blank. I stood on stage for thirty seconds, looking down, just mumbling "Sorry" and "Wow."

"I remember," Laura said, sharing my pain.

"On the plus side, it was after that night that I knew I could do comedy," I offered.

"You bombing meant you could do comedy?" she asked.

"Kind of. I realized that's about the worst you can possibly do in a stand-up show," I said. "And it sucked. But I also didn't die. And I figured I could only go up from there. I also stopped memorizing my set word for word and start working off a set-list instead."

Laura smiled a "we've all been there" smile.

"Well, I look forward to performing together in another ten years," I said with a laugh.

"Me too," Laura agreed. "Although, I heard there's another comedy show nearby at a place called fooBAR that we could probably get on. Justin and I were thinking about going."

Two shows in one night with an old comedy pal? Sign me up. Plus it'd give me a chance to test out some new material I had just thought of. "I met two different people with pet flying squirrels today. That's nuts!"

9. ALABAMA

Rocket Man-child
Huntsville, AL. May 19, 2015

I started to get self-conscious. I knew I stuck out like that stray hair your barber always seems to miss or that one tile in your bathroom that's rotated the wrong way. Maybe it was a mistake to come.

I imagined people were looking at me and thinking, "What is he doing here?" I was the sore thumb, the black sheep, the odd man out, the 501st wheel, the "adult who was at a kid's museum by himself on a Tuesday morning." I felt that way mostly because I was the adult who was at a kid's museum by himself on a Tuesday morning. Specifically, I was at the US Space and Rocket Center in Huntsville, Alabama, and I was surrounded by people two feet shorter than me and twenty years younger.

I was in the second state of my current road trip and had done stand up the night before at a bar called Maggie Meyer's Irish Pub. I was headed to Mississippi next, but first I had to complete my Alabama activity.

Deciding what I wanted to do in the Heart of Dixie had been a no-brainer. When I was growing up, every other year my family would visit my grandmother in Gulf Shores. Every other year, on our drive down I-65, we would pass the giant rocket that sits outside the US Space and Rocket Center near Huntsville. Every other year, I would dream of one day going inside.

It was now that day. I awoke that morning with a spring in my step, a swag in my sway, and a sense of joy emanating from my body.

However, when I arrived, my swagful sway swayed away. I quickly realized I was the only adult there of their own volition. Anyone over the age of twelve was only there because they worked there, they were a chaperone, or they were a parent or grandparent. Everyone else in the museum was a kid.

I took a deep breath to strengthen my resolve. Who cares that I was the only adult willingly at the space museum? Kids don't get to have a monopoly on learning more about space exploration and pretending to be an astronaut space cowboy.

As I walked around, I acted nonchalant about my interest in the various exhibitions. Oh, a room explaining how telescopes work and pictures from Hubble? Interesting. An entire wing dedicated to the different trips to the moon? Isn't that swell. What's that? A Tilt-a-Whirl-like ride that lets you experience 3Gs?

Holy wow, it was a Tilt-a-Whirl ride that lets you experience 3Gs. In a burst of excitement, I ran to get in line for the G-Force Accelerator and, as I filed in behind two ten-year-olds, I remembered that I was the outcast.

I looked around to see who was judging me and, to my surprise, no one seemed to care. The kids were too engrossed with the museum, the teenage workers were too engrossed with each other, and the parents were too engrossed in their phones or in wrangling their demon children. No one noticed the adult at a kid's museum on a Tuesday morning.

I began to wonder why I was so concerned in the first place. As the talented James Bailey tells his improv students, "If you ever start to feel self-conscious, just remember, nobody cares about you."

He doesn't mean it in a "you're all alone" kind of way, but more that people are so entwined in their own lives that they hardly stop to think about someone else's. And the people who spend their time judging you probably aren't people you should care about getting judged by anyway.

Besides, why should a space museum be reserved for just kids and their handlers? For that matter, why were playgrounds, video games, and having a temper tantrum now and then just for kids? Last I checked, there was no age limit on having fun, no expiration date on play, and no reason to become a poopy-pants party pooper just because you reached a certain milestone. Getting older doesn't mean you have to get old. So what if you have a "serious job" or have "so much work to do." You can't take ten minutes to swing on a swing set or jump in a puddle?

In many ways, I've never fully grown up. Not in my diet, my hobbies, or my mentality (I still laugh when I hear the word *duty*). Maybe it's because of my work, or because I was a Toys R Us kid, or maybe it's because the notion of what it means to be an adult is skewed.

As a kid, adults are those people who have all the answers, they don't get nervous or make mistakes, and they certainly don't have fun. They are authority figures that are far too serious. But as you get older, you realize none of those things are true.

There is no magic switch, no age when you instantly feel like an adult. You just keep getting older, then one day, *poof*, some kid you thought of as a peer calls you "sir," and the illusion is destroyed. You realize the person you're talking to was born after significant moments in your life, born after 1990 when the Cincinnati Reds won the World Series or after 1998 when *Animaniacs*, *Bill Nye the Science Guy*, and *Seinfeld* all went off the air.

But despite the fact I was now into my third decade, I didn't *feel* like an adult. And maybe that's because I still do kid things. I have an *I'm Still a Kid* party every year for my birthday,[32] I still high-five people because it's way cooler than a handshake, and I'm not entirely sure my voice ever dropped.

But is any of that bad? Most of the implicit restrictions of being an adult don't make sense anyway. Why is drinking a cocktail a mature thing to do, but drinking Kool-Aid is for children? Why is it okay to binge watch reality TV, but playing a video game is a waste of time? Why can an adult pretend to know what they're doing with their life, but they can't pretend to be an action hero when the urge strikes?

As the line started to move and twenty kids and I strapped into the ride, I decided that being an adult meant getting to decide what you want to do, no matter what age it was originally intended for. Sure, there's plenty of research on how humor and play reduce stress, improve productivity, and increase creativity, but why not have a little fun just for fun's sake?

I buckled up and braced myself. The G-Force Accelerator started spinning, first like the Tea Cups in Disney World, then like a dryer in its final cycle, and finally like a Tilt-a-Whirl on steroids, stopping just short of the speed that would seemingly cause your brain to leak out of your ears. I felt slightly disheveled, a little dizzy, and ludicrously happy—so I rode it again.

For the rest of my visit, I didn't care what anyone else thought. I rode the Space Shot (also twice), played a jetpack simulation game, and had fun with various gizmos and gadgets galore.

After three hours of wonderful playtime, I made my way toward the exit. As I was leaving, I caught sight of an astronaut spacesuit with the helmet visor removed so you could get a picture of what you might look like as a space cowboy. A mother had just finished taking pictures of her two daughters in the suit as I walked up.

---

32 These parties are the best. You have people over and tell them to bring something they enjoyed eating or drinking as a kid. Then you all go to munchtown on Bagel Bites, Fruit by the Foot, and Big League Chew while drinking Capri Suns and chocolate milk, working your way into a sugar high that will lead to a sugar hangover the next day. It's fantastic.

Without hesitating, I asked if she would mind taking my picture in the suit. The woman obliged, and I stepped into a childhood fantasy with a giant grin on my face. If she was judging me for being a thirty-one-year-old man in the US Space and Rocket Center by himself, she didn't show it on her face. But more importantly, I wouldn't have cared if she did.[33]

---

33 Check out the incredible picture at tarv.in/alabama

10. MISSISSIPPI

The Walmart Sleeping Lot
Jackson, MS. May 19, 2015

I pulled into the lot a little after 22:30. A few cars were clustered near the front of the store; a few others were scattered across the parking area. The whole thing looked like a chessboard with one side losing badly. I decided that this would do. I'd arrived at my hotel for the night: the parking lot of a Walmart somewhere near Jackson, Mississippi.

During my travels, I would stay in some incredible places. There was the fancy hotel in Savannah that had a luxurious bathtub, the floor-to-ceiling windowed suite in Las Vegas, and the three-star room that had a five-star view of Denali in Anchorage. I would also crash on people's couches, rent out rooms via Airbnb, and sleep on planes and trains while en route to my next destination.

And, now, I was about to add "parking lot" to the list.

I had just finished a stand-up show at a place called Fenian's Pub nearby and wanted to stay in the area. In the morning, I was going to visit the Vicksburg National Military Park, a historical site that preserves what Lincoln called "the key" to the Union's victory, but I was too tired to make the drive.

I couldn't find a reasonably priced hotel, so I elected to stay the night in Hotel Rental Car @ Walmart. I certainly could have gotten a hotel, but I refused to pay $150 for a room in Jackson when I've paid two-thirds of that in better cities.[34] Besides, what's a nomadic trip without the "sleeping in a car" experience? A much better trip, actually.

I chose a Walmart because I remembered when comedian Chris Gethard made his cross-country RV trip, he mentioned the store had a policy that allowed people to stay overnight (in the parking lot; you weren't allowed to sleep on the bean bag chairs in the toys department—I tried). So, I figured if he could do it, I could manage it as well. One key difference I didn't take into account: he had an RV; I had a Ford Fiesta.

As far as hotel accommodations go, Walmart doesn't have the greatest amenities: there is a shared bathroom but no showers, they don't have a workout room despite having lots of workout equipment, and there is no Wi-Fi signal in some of the more remote "rooms." But they do have an incredible mini-fridge selection; you just have to go to the lobby to get it.

Overall, they're also pretty safe. Most WPLs (Walmart parking lots) have security cameras, and some of the better (or perhaps worse) ones have a security team that patrols at night. The only thing you do have to watch out for is falling prices.[35]

The rooms themselves are entirely dependent on what you drove up in. My room, the Ford Fiesta, was one of the smaller options with two half-single beds (with safety harnesses), a trunk closet, and a safety deposit box that was supposed to store gloves but more often contained registration info and napkins.

I pulled my room into a parking spot about halfway across the lot from the entrance. I wanted to be near a light for safety but not directly under one so I could sleep easier. I looked around at my sleeping quarters. This wouldn't be so bad. In fact, it may even be kind of fun.

I went to the lobby to grab some snacks, and then came back to my car and did a little research.

I googled "How to sleep in a car" and was met with some surprisingly helpful results. Among the most useful: don't sleep in the driver's seat (there's more stuff in the way making it less comfortable); crack two catty-cornered windows for ventilation; and have a bigger car if possible.

Despite my research, I made a couple of rookie mistakes that negatively impacted my parking lot lodging. The biggest was that I had forgotten to confirm that the Walmart was of the twenty-four-hour variety. This one wasn't.

I wrapped up my research and random interneting a little after midnight and looked up from my phone just in time to see some employees lock-

---

34 Okay, maybe better is too strong of a word. The City of Jackson was very pleasant, but when one of your claims to fame on Wikipedia is that you were mentioned in a Bruno Mars song, you might not be the most exciting of metropolises.

35 This joke brought to you by *Walmart*®.

ing the front doors to customers. Dagnabbit! I hadn't brushed my teeth yet and needed to use the bathroom. Unless I wanted to pretend like a cart pusher who was just really late for his shift, I wasn't going to be able to do either of those things here.

Not to be deterred, I brought up Google Maps and found a nearby gas station.

I started up my room and arrived at the gas station two minutes later. I grabbed my toothpaste and brush from my luggage and headed inside. All of the late-night adjustments my eyes had gone through from the dim lighting of my car were immediately destroyed by the industrial fluorescents lights of the station.

As I headed toward the sign of the little man, I remembered what gas station bathrooms were like. I hid my dental care supplies in my pocket and entered the porcelain chamber. My reservations were confirmed. The bathroom reeked of awfulness and had a look to match. I decided to skip the "brushing my teeth part" for the night, as it seemed dirtier to open my mouth than to go the night without the minty cleaning.

I finished up and headed back to the WPL, electing for a different room location. The last one was a bit too bright so I parked a little further away, but not so far away that it was easily accessed by creatures of the night.

I cracked the windows on the driver's side and back right seat, and climbed over the console ottoman into my bed. I reclined the seat, took off my shoes, and rolled my hoodie into a pillow. I folded my arms over my chest and went to sleep.

I woke up a few times to turn the car on briefly to get the air going, change the crackage of the windows, try different sleeping positions, check the time, curse my decision to not get a hotel, adjust my pillow, try other different sleeping positions, peek out into the parking lot to make sure there were no creatures, and re-curse my decision not to get a hotel. But in between those moments, I got some rest.

I awoke at 06:30 in the morning, dull-eyed and flat-tailed. My back ached, my neck was sore, and I felt like I might be getting sick. I could taste my own breath, and it was not good. The sun taunted my emotional state through the windows, welcoming me to the day with a nice, bright "F you, buddy!"

I told myself this was all just part of the nomadic lifestyle, that this experience was adding to the scope of the journey. All it really did was make me long for having a home again (or at least a $150 hotel room). Being a nomad was great as long as you didn't have to sacrifice anything. Had I been more awake, I might have wondered if it was all worth it; instead, I just thought about food.

I got out of my acute-angled bed and made my way into the now-open lobby. I brushed my teeth, went to the bathroom, and grabbed a box of Pop Tarts. I went for the Cookies & Cream variety because even if I didn't have a great night's sleep, I could at least have a great breakfast.

Ten Tips for Sleeping in a Car

My best suggestion for sleeping in a car is don't. You can't find a reasonably priced hotel? You don't have a friend of a friend you can crash with? What about a hostel?

No? Well, if you're certain you want to do this, here are ten tips to make the best of the situation:

1. Find a quiet but secure area to park. Walmart parking lots tend to work, as do the driveways of a family member's place where you can sleep inside.

2. Pick a parking spot that isn't so bright that you won't be able to sleep but isn't so dark that it's unsafe. The right amount of light is about the same as what you would have if you were sleeping at an Airbnb and they had a night-light for you.

3. Determine which direction the sun will rise so you can angle the car away from it. Otherwise you'll wake up naturally when the sun starts beating down on you unless you get one of those sunshades that act as curtains, those things they have in most motels.

4. Try to maintain as much of your normal going-to-bed ritual as possible. Find a spot where you can brush your teeth and go to the bathroom before you settle in. Hostels tend to have these amenities in a room right next to a room you can sleep in.

5. Keep the car doors locked but crack two windows slightly to allow airflow. Kind of like the airflow you might get from an AC, heater, or fan in a friend's place you might crash at.

6. Make sure you have something to serve as a blanket and something to serve as a pillow. I recommend an actual blanket and an actual pillow in a hotel room.

7. Sleep in the passenger seat or in the back to give yourself more room away from pedals and the steering wheel, two things rooms at an inn tend to be free of.

8. Try different positions to see what is most comfortable. It could be on your back, curled into a ball, or in a bed.

9. Say, "Goodnight, moon."

10. Have water to drink when you wake up. It will help you shake off the groggy feeling in the morning. Sleeping in a bed and waking up to continental breakfast can serve the same purpose.

I hope these tips help you the next time you find yourself in a situation where you have to sleep in a car. Really? You can't even find a cheap Motel 6?

11. ARKANSAS

No Money, Mo Problems
Little Rock, AR. May 20, 2015

Traveling can be expensive. First, you have the cost of getting to your destination; then you have the cost of transportation once you're there. Next is the cost of your place to stay, the cost of food, and any type of entertainment. And of course, the cost of buying yet another pair of fingernail clippers because you keep losing them.

There are ways you can make the whole process cheaper: you can use loyalty programs to amass travel miles or free stays, find ways to justify your travel as a business expense so that it can be written off when it comes to taxes,[36] and stop losing fingernail clippers.

But the reality is, in order to travel, you need money. And as I made my way through Arkansas, I had none. Or rather, I had money; I just had no way to access it. I was currently in Little Rock, while my wallet was currently in my hotel room, forty-five miles away in Pine Falls. I had stopped there earlier in the day to nap and prep for the show and left my wallet on the dresser right next to the overpriced bottle of water and my enthusiasm for this trip.

I was tired, sick, and in desperate need of sustenance. I hadn't eaten anything in the last eight hours since the Pop Tart I had for breakfast, and I still hadn't recovered from car sleep the night before. And now I was just thirty minutes away from my show that night, and I was getting so hangry that I was

---

36 This one is highly underrated. Thanks to this book, my travels were technically research.

willing to use the terrible portmanteau of hungry + angry.

Normally I'm pretty good about taking everything with me—thanks to the classic triple pat check for phone, wallet, and keys—but I wasn't feeling well and had left in a rush because I wanted to see Big Dam Bridge, a tourist attraction that is a big dam bridge, before going to my show.

Admittedly, the Big Dam Bridge was beautiful. It consisted of a long concrete walkway that climbed its way up and across the Murray Lock and Dam that regulated the waters of the Arkansas River. I had arrived just in time to catch the sunset adding an orange Cheetos crust to the water below. The scene was picturesque, so I took a few pictures and more than one selfie.

But visiting the dam meant I was now sans money, sans food, and sans time. I couldn't go back to get my wallet because I wouldn't make it back in time for the show. I couldn't skip the show because this was the only time I was going to be in Arkansas, and I still needed to perform there. And I couldn't just eat after the show because I didn't know how long it would last, I would still have a forty-five-minute drive back, and I was fairly sure I was going to die of starvation (or at least a bad mood).

I drove the streets of suburban Little Rock and wondered if this stupid trip was worth it. What was I trying to prove? That I could survive out on my own? I survived seven years in NYC and, to be Frank, if I can make it there, I can make it anywhere. It's not like I was backpacking the Appalachian Trail or going into the wild.

In my food-deprived state, I considered moving back to NYC after this trip. Three months as a nomad was respectable, and having a home base would simplify things. And hopefully, it would prevent me from being in situations like this: sick, tired, hungry, and penniless.

I felt a sense of relief knowing I wouldn't be a nomad forever and decided to get laser (pew pew!) focused on the task at hand. The only way to prevent my physical/mental starvation was to figure out a way to buy food with what I had with me.

I pulled the car to the side of the road in a nondescript neighborhood and took inventory of everything I had on my person: my phone, my back-pack, and my rental car. The glove compartment contained nothing remotely useful; the center console housed my EZ Pass and iPod; the trunk was empty save for the spare tire and a sock that I did not put there.

A search of my backpack yielded my computer, voice recorder, head-phones, mints, aspirin, notebook, titanium spork, and—wait a second—three stray checks. Paper checks that in the olden days could be cashed for real money. Yes, I was somehow in the situation where I had checks on me but not credit cards or cash, something that hasn't been true for anyone since 1995.

I googled nearby banks, but they were all closed as it was now nearing 19:00 and who could possibly have to do any banking outside of standard business hours? So, I tried grocery stores and found a Kroger close by.

I quickly made my way there, walked confidently into the store, to the Customer Service counter, and triumphantly asked if I could write them a check to be cashed. They said no.

Well, first they said, "Do you have any ID?" I said, "No." Then they said, "No."

I hadn't anticipated that no wallet meant no driver's license and no driver's license meant no way of proving my identity which meant no cashier was willing to exchange their green paper with a president on it for my tan paper with my address on it.

I returned to my car and considered my options. I decided my best chance for food would be at The Afterthought, the bar where the open mic was. My hope was that the place might be on the cutting edge of payment technology with Google Wallet, PayPal, Venmo, Facebook Payments, or in-app purchases.

So I ignited tiny explosions in my car by starting the engine, and made my way to the bar. When I arrived, I found a server and asked if they took digital currency. She looked at me as if I had said citigal durrency or any other combination of sounds that make zero sense. She said no but that they did take credit card. The hope that I might ever eat again began to wane.

I was at the venue, so there was no point in leaving. Instead, I looked around for inspiration. An intricate mural lined the walls, depicting the scene of an outdoor cafe with musicians playing on the street. I could try busking perhaps? Oh, wait, no, I had no musical talent to busk, and this was a music open mic where people who were actually talented would be playing for free.

I could try begging, either of the venue or the people in the bar, but that involved talking to strangers, and I decided I'd rather starve. I had resigned myself to just eating pieces of napkins when the phone rang at the bar. I saw the server answer it and take an order for pickup. I had an idea.

I got the server's attention and asked if she could enter my credit card using just the credit card number but not the card itself. Her response was skepticism. I explained the situation and added a dollop of Drew Tarvin Charm™, and she became more skeptical.

She said she couldn't technically do that in the restaurant, but if I were placing an order over the phone and wanted to pay by card, she could take the numbers that way. Hmm, a little bit of kindness mixed with a gray area for business practices? That worked for me—assuming I knew the numbers on my credit card.

I wish I could say I had a memory palace like Sherlock Holmes and that my credit card number was represented by the number of GI Joes sitting in various spots in my mind, but I don't.

I did have the next best thing though: access to the internet. I took out my phone, logged into my bank account, and checked my online statement. It only showed the last four digits of my card for what I am assuming is security purposes. I clicked through every link I could find until I stumbled on the PDF version of a paper statement that showed my credit card number completely in the buff. I felt reassured that if a hacker somehow got into my account, they would surely never think to check the PDFs.

I called the bar from where I was sitting inside the bar. I desperately wanted the server to scream, "The call is coming from inside the house!" *ala* the movie *Scream,* but she did not.

She took the call and pretended she wasn't looking at me as I gave my order. I told her my card number and gave her my zip code. If she had asked for the CVC code on the back, I would have been screwed. I smiled at her and hung up.

Twenty minutes later the food came out, and I was able to eat—right after I got off stage because I was up next to perform. I did my set to a moderately okay response, but I didn't care; my primary focus was food.

I sat back down at my high top and chowed down on my club sandwich. As I ate, a man on guitar played a cover of a James Taylor song, and my mood started to lift. I was still sick and tired, but only in the literal sense, not the figurative. I was no longer hungry or angry or using portmanteaus.

I felt like Scarlett O'Hara from *Gone with the Wind,* "I'm going to live through this, and when it's all over, I'll never be hungry again. So long as I don't leave my wallet in my hotel room, I'll never be hungry again."

12. LOUISIANA

Pull!
Sunshine, LA. May 22, 2015

I looked down the scope of the long-barreled shotgun. The butt of the gun pressed against my left shoulder, my right eye closed for focus, my left finger on the trigger.

Josue counted down "3 . . . 2 . . . 1 . . . Pull!"

The orange disk flew. I tracked it with the barrel of the gun and pulled the trigger.

Bang!

The disk exploded in the air. I had an inexplicable desire to curse, but there were kids around, so I let out a "Yeeeeee hawwwwww!"

I was just outside of Baton Rouge, Louisiana, in a town called Sunshine, at my brother's (David) friend's (Sarah) mom's place. As part of my current road trip, I was meeting David in Louisiana before we both continued on to Gulf Shores to meet my other brother, Adam, his girlfriend, Leanne, and my mom, Mom, for a vacation at my grandmother's place. But for now, we were capping off a busy day with something I had never done before: shooting a gun.

Earlier that day, after I finished some work and recorded an interview, David, Sarah, and I had gone adventuring. I wanted to go the original Raising Canes, an incredible chicken finger restaurant that started in Baton Rouge, but on our drive in, we had seen some ruins on a nearby farm and decided that we wanted to take pictures instead. To be more accurate, David and Sarah saw the ruins and decided they wanted to take pictures in front of them so they could Photoshop a Dragon into it. I wanted Canes sauce.[37]

The ruins, of course, were on private property, a farm owned by a person Sarah had never met. A fence kept the farmer's cows in and trespassers out. Not to be deterred by clear signs of "Do NOT ENTER," we searched for a way in.

We walked along the fence to see if we could find a gate but had no such luck. We considered just hopping over it, but we were unsure if it was electrified. David picked a long piece of grass and touched it to the fence. His eyes grew wide as he let out a yelp and pulled the grass away. Yes, the fence was electric (Boogie Woogie Woogie).

The fence was too high to jump, so we tried to find a spot where we could crawl under. We found such a location that wasn't too muddy and, one by one, trespassed our way onto the farm. My heart was racing as I lowered myself all the way to the ground, barely lifting myself to shimmy underneath. I was afraid that I might accidentally raise my badonkadonk and get electrocuted, even though my badonkadonk is quite small. I just didn't want to imagine what a current intended to keep massive bovine at bay would do to something that weighed 140 pounds.

We all three made it under without incident and made our way to the ruins. The only things remaining of whatever it used to be were pillars of red brick, gray concrete, and the definition of foliage. We had no idea what it had been for, but we knew its purpose now: future dragon pictures. We took roughly one thousand photos with David and Sarah in various poses, leaving enough room for the would-be Khaleesi pet.

As my subjects readied for another pose, I noticed that a herd of cows had seen that we were there. The source of an essential ingredient to chocolate milk looked at us much like a group of bikers might look at someone showing up to their biker bar on a unicycle: confused and not necessarily happy.

We continued taking pictures when a few cows started making their way toward us. I can't really read cow micro expressions and know very little about the creatures other than their udder need to be milked,[38] but my guess was that they weren't thinking, "These people look nice; let's go greet them," but rather, "Who is trespassing on our land, and why don't we kill them?"

We decided not to stick around to find out their intentions and made our way back to the fence, but not before I stepped in a "mud pie" just to round out the trespassing experience. We climbed under and returned to Sarah's place, where in her front yard, her stepdad, Josue, was loading a shotgun.

---

37 Fortunately we had Canes the next day as we headed toward Florida.
38 You're welcome.

At first I thought he was mad we had snuck onto someone else's property, but instead, he had set up a skeet shooter so we could fire off some firearms. And not just us, but the whole family, including Sarah's boyfriend Chuck and his two kids.

The only weapons I had ever previously used had Nerf written on the side of them, so I decided this was just as good a time as any to shoot my first real gun. I figured it would be fun, add a story to my list, and bolster my skillset should a zombie apocalypse ever break out:

- Can I drive a stick shift? Yes. Motorcycle? Not yet.
- Can I start a fire? Yes. Without matches or a lighter? No.
- Can I shoot a gun? Probably. Can I hit the things I shoot at? TBD.

I started out with the pistol grip shotgun, which I would later discover made my thumb muscle sore. I wasn't sure what it said about my manhood that simply pulling a trigger could cause muscle aches, but it certainly didn't raise my perception of my manliness.

I wasn't very good with the pistol grip, so I switched to the long-barreled shotgun. I also started out shooting right-handed. From what I can tell, or at least approximate with the finger trick, I'm left-handed but right-eyed, and supposedly the eye is more important. I went 0 for 15 shooting that way, so I tried the other side.

And that's when the magic happened. I hit my first target, then my second. I missed one and then hit two more. After each successful hit, I let out a cliché phrase of excitement often found in bad Western films: "Hoo doggie," "Yippee kay yay," "Sweet tea!"

After a few more trigger pulls, the sun started to set so we packed everything up. We grilled up some steak and chicken and ate like kings. I pretended the food we were eating was the result of my shooting. Victory tasted sweet.

I felt re-energized about my trip. Being with people I knew and expanding my horizons reminded me of why I loved traveling in the first place.

I decided to postpone any thoughts of cutting my nomadic journey short. As long as I stayed healthy, didn't leave valuable resources in my hotel room, and made sure to do energizing activities along the way, I could do this.

And, if a zombie apocalypse ever did occur, I knew exactly what I'd do. I'd find a long-barreled shotgun, hop in a sports car, and drive to Sunshine, Louisiana where I'd wait out the brain-eating epidemic nestled up to some angry cows.

13. FLORIDA

My First Poetry Show
Pensacola, FL. May 26, 2015

I stepped up to the microphone and looked out over the audience. Red Christmas lights hung from the ceiling with a sole spotlight illuminating my figure against a white backdrop. Audience members sat at small round tables in the middle of the space or on barstools along the side. My family sat in the back, making up some of the only white faces in the crowd.

We were at a slam poetry show, and most of the audience had turned up to see the incredibly talented Shelton Alexander aka "African American Shakespear" aka "Shake," a poet based in New Orleans with a commanding voice and even more commanding control of the English language. But first, there were a few other poets doing readings, one of whom was me.

After my gun-shooting adventure in Louisiana, David and I had driven to Gulf Shores to meet up with family for an early summer vacation. While in the area, I was able to find a weekly poetry show at a vegan restaurant called Sluggo's in nearby Pensacola that could count as my Florida performance. The only problem was, up until that point, I had never done any spoken word (save for a wedding reading I did at my cousin's wedding a couple of years ago). But, when I inquired about the show, I mentioned I was a comic from New York City who also did spoken word, and they agreed to give me some time on the stage (clearly not fact checking any of my claims).

I was grateful for the opportunity but also deeply nervous.

Though I had done over 900 improv and stand-up shows at that point, every performance type is different. The expectations of a spoken word crowd are quite different than that of improv or stand-up. In improv, the audience knows you're making things up on the spot, so the bar for laughter is lower since it's created in the moment, just for them. Stand-up audiences tend to have higher expectations, sometimes to the point it feels like they're thinking, "You think you're funny? Prove it." Spoken word audiences don't care if you make them laugh, but they do want you to make them feel. Quite the challenge for an emotionally stunted robot.

As I approached the mic, the audience seemed to be thinking, "What is this white boy going to say?" I was wondering the same thing.

I introduced myself and started with my first bit, or I guess in poetry, what they call the first reading.

"Hello everyone, my name is Drew Tarvin, and with this performance, I will have performed in the thirteenth state of my tour."

There was a light round of applause.

"The first thing I'd like to start with is a dramatic reading of dumb jokes." I cleared my throat and attempted to lower my voice to add some semblance of drama.

"I saw a man smoking outside, so I went up to him and asked 'Is that a cigarette you're smoking?' . . . He said, 'Close, but no, cigar.'"

There was a long pause followed by polite laughter. I began to wonder if I was cut out for poetry. Maybe I was too far out of my element; maybe this was the limit of my performance abilities. But it was too late; there was nothing I could do but proceed to the next dumb joke.

"I feel like windshield wiper fluid is the most gangsta part of the car . . . because it's from the 'hood."

This time there was a much louder reaction of laughter. I felt encouraged. I continued through a few more dumb jokes, some doing well and others leaving the crowd quiet.

I finished with my favorite joke.

"I was at the airport when the man in front of me tried to control his child while checking into his flight. The flight agent asked: 'Your son is quite unruly. Do you want to check him with your bags?' The man replied, 'Thanks, but I think I'll carry on my wayward son.'"

A slow laugh spread across the room, not great but not bad. I transitioned into my second reading.

"For the next piece, I want to talk about something a little less dramatic: the meaning of life."

It was a piece I called "The Clichéd Meaning of Life." I had written it for stand-up a long time ago but decided to dust it off, as it was the most spoken wordy thing I had ever worked on.

I made some substantial changes to it: tweaks to the flow, additional clichés, and a through line attempting to discover what matters most. It was a lot stronger than before, but I didn't have the new version memorized, which meant I had to read it off my phone. This would be death at a stand-up club, but it was standard at a poetry show for newer poets.

The piece starts out with an introduction and then launches into one hundred clichés in four minutes, exploring the meaning of life. As I went through the poem, there were pauses for laughter, some head nodding, and I received my first "Mmh!" from the crowd.

It was the first time I had ever received that nonverbal but vocal confirmation, announcing that someone agreed with what I said on an emotional level. As a comedian, I definitely live for laughter, but that "mmh" and accompanying snaps were something I didn't know I had been longing for. I finished the bit to loud applause and stepped offstage, getting an approving handshake from the host.

"That was Drew, uh . . . well, Drew, ladies and gentleman," the host said as I walked off stage. I didn't know this but a lot of poets use nicknames for their shows (a la "African American Shakespear") and so the host was a bit surprised with the simplicity of my moniker.

I went to the back and sat with my family, receiving glowing reviews from all of them. As the other poets performed, I marveled at the energy of the room and emotion of their work. Some were incredible with wordplay, others with their commitment to performance; some weren't very good at all. The audience was engaged and supportive of all of these artists revealing some of their deepest inner thoughts.

As the evening wound down and "Shake" left us mesmerized and inspired by his words, I reflected on the experience.

There's something special about your first time doing anything—your first kiss, your first time driving a car, your first draft of a book detailing your travels to all the states. The first time is rarely perfect, but it is usually memorable. But too often we're scared to try new things out of fear of being bad at them. But if we only did things we knew we wouldn't fail at, we'd all still be crawling around on our hands and knees because we fell down the first time we tried to walk. And getting past those first times is the only way to discover new passions, new hobbies, and new worlds.

I still had plenty more firsts to come on my trip: my first time eating rattlesnake (Colorado), my first time taking a helicopter ride (Arizona), and my first time touching a Ferrari (California). But that first poetry show was something surreal.

I never knew that, as an engineer, I would thoroughly enjoy such an emotionally driven art form. Perhaps I was drawn to it because it was so different. Or maybe I liked that they were accepting of wordplay and puns, so long as they were attached to a greater message. All I knew is that I had experienced a new culture and found a new interest thanks to my nomadic journey. This had been by first poetry show but it certainly wouldn't be my last.

Now I just needed to come up with a good nickname. Drupac maybe? Drucifer? I got it: Winnie the Drew.

The Clichéd Meaning of Life

This is the full poem I shared at a number of venues during my journey.[39]

Have you ever seen a performance so inspirational, gone through a breakup so challenging, or had a milkshake that was so delicious . . . you started to contemplate the meaning of life? It's something I've been thinking about a lot lately—the meaning of life. Maybe the meaning of life is money . . .

As they say money makes the world go 'round . . .
Yet they also say the best things in life are free.
So do you live free or die hard?
Cuz to make ends meet
You have to start rollin' in the dough.
But doe, a deer, a female deer . . .
Is nothing when the buck stops right here.
And I ain't saying she's a gold digger,
But mo money mo problems,
So you better check yourself before you wreck yourself,
Because money can't buy happiness.
But don't worry, be happy,
And live happily ever after
In a land far far away
Where there's light at the end of the tunnel.
And to pass with flying colors,
Don't color outside the lines
But think outside the box.
I don't want to go off on a tangent
But things don't add up
If it's the thought that counts
And it's better to give than to receive
Then sharing is caring.
But Jimmy crack corn and I don't care,
Because crack is whack
And it's hugs not drugs,
So put that in your pipe and smoke it.
But do you just say no
Or do you just do it?
If impossible is nothing,

---

39 To see the performance of this piece, check out the video at tarv.in/clichepoetry

Then a mission impossible
Ain't nothing but a g thang, baby.
So stop, collaborate, and listen.

Because maybe the meaning of life isn't money; maybe the meaning of life is
knowledge.

Because knowledge is power
And with great power comes great responsibility,
So don't just drink responsibly, but think responsibly,
Because I know what you did last summer.
And knowing is half the battle.
But is it a battle of the wits
Or a battle to the death?
Is the pen mightier than the sword,
Or is it a sword in the stone,
That can break my bones, when words will never hurt me.
Because I'm rubber and you're glue, so whatever you say bounces off me and
sticks to you
So speak now or forever hold your peace.
And don't judge a book by its cover,
Because beauty is only skin deep.
And if looks can kill
And I wear my heart on my sleeve,
Then I'm armed and dangerous.
And home is where the heart is
And there's no place like home,
Sweet home, Alabama.
But that's just my state of mind
In this state of denial
Of the status quo.
I say carpe diem
If it's quid pro quo
Get yourself tit for tat,
And break me off a piece of that.
So eat great, even late
Because if you're hungry, why wait?
Except patience is a virtue,
So don't stop believin' but
Stop, in the name of love.

Because maybe the meaning life isn't money or knowledge; maybe the meaning of life is love.

What's love got to do with it? (Got to do with it?)
Well, love conquers all,
And even if you've lost that loving' feeling,
Know that it's better to have loved and lost than to never have loved at all.
Because there are plenty of fish in the sea,
And when Love is in the air
You'll be walking on cloud nine.
But when it rains it pours,
And if you're under the weather
And can't see through the fog
We may not see eye-to-eye.
If love is blind
And hindsight is 20/20,
Then is love at first sight
Really meant to be?
Or not to be? That's the question.
And if you've got question, we've got answers,
If you can do it, we can help,
Because when you're here, you're family,
And family matters
As you step by step
Through the wonder years.
Because what goes up, must come down,
What goes around, comes around.
There's nothing to fear but fear itself.
To live and learn
You have to crash and burn,
And the only failure is quitting.
So what are you waiting for?
To have the time of your life.
You have to find the time
To live a life worth living
So stop, hammertime.

Maybe the meaning of life isn't money, knowledge, or love. Maybe the meaning of life is to find meaning in life. Or maybe it's milkshakes; I don't know.

14. SOUTH CAROLINA

South of the Border
Hamer, SC. May 28, 2015

I was driving north on I-95 in South Carolina, rocking out to some Taylor Swift (don't judge me), when I passed the first sign. My eyes caught a brief glimpse of it against the sky-blue plains overhead.

It read: "SOUTH OF THE BORDER."

I was back on the road after a four-day break for a family vacation in Alabama and Florida. I did a show in Columbia, South Carolina, the night before and was now headed to Pennsylvania to speak at a conference. It was a beautiful spring day, the sun preached overhead in the noon sky.

I thought little of the sign until a few miles later when I spotted another one, then another and another. Before long, I had passed a comically high number of billboards, like what you might see in a Road Runner cartoon when Wile E. is trying to convince you that there is a tunnel ahead. They all referenced SOUTH OF THE BORDER.

We've all been in this predicament: traveling along, going from Point A to Point B when suddenly something catches our eye, and we have to decide whether to go out of our way to check out Point D.[40] So often we pass these things when we're in a rush, and we don't have the opportunity to stop; we don't get to see where the side quests might lead. But I was a nomad; I could stop.

---

40 You know, take a D tour.

Granted, I still had eight hours of driving until I got to Philadelphia, but I wasn't in any immediate rush. And after my efficiency realization in Maine, I was trying to be better at enjoying the states as I traveled through them, and this might be a chance to do that in South Carolina. Plus I was intrigued by the approximately one billion billboards I passed, and I wanted to know more.

So, as I neared the North Carolina border, I pulled off at Exit 1 and found a parking spot in front of a souvenir shop. I crossed the street to take a selfie with the giant SOUTH OF THE BORDER sign and was about to head back when I noticed the first statue. It was an orange giraffe with oddly muscular legs that seemed randomly placed as though movers had set it there temporarily and then forgot it existed.

I took a few pictures and continued back to my car when I saw another statue, this one of a twenty-foot tall gorilla wearing a blue t-shirt. I took another photo and then saw yet another statue. Then another statue, then another, and then the one that confirmed what I was beginning to suspect: South of the Border wasn't just a kitschy roadside attraction. It was the tackiest, weirdest, and most offensive Americana rest stop in the country.

The confirming statue was a Golliwog-esque representation of a Mexican man in a sombrero. It appeared to be the South of the Border mascot, cheering on that this place was either offensively ignorant or openly racist.

I now fully understood the name: the place was just south of the North Carolina border, but the theme was everything a *Family Guy* episode might portray as south of the US border.

I walked to the car, determined to leave the ignorance behind. Then I saw a statue of a giant T-rex and was torn. I didn't want to support a business that was unabashedly stereotypical, but I also didn't want to miss out on taking a picture of a giant T-rex.

When I started my journey to see all fifty states, I wanted to see what the entire country had to offer. That meant seeing the good, the bad, and the tacky. I wasn't condoning the prejudices of others; I was just reporting on what existed. And if I was there as what was essentially an investigative photojournalist, it was my right, nay, my responsibility, to research things further. So I did.

My eyes scanned my surroundings to take it all in. It was like a small town, containing everything you needed, just in slightly offensive fashion. There was a gas station, hotel, and four or five restaurants, including one shaped like an enormous sombrero. There was also a campground, access to a BMX park, and a tall sombrero tower that was under construction, presumably to add more nachos to its decor.

There were also countless stores, some of convenience, many others of souvenir. The souvenir shops were filled with everything any souvenir shop had ever carried, anywhere. Each store had a very loose theme and thousands of things you would give away for free at a garage sale.

One store had an entire section dedicated to beach accessories, despite being sixty miles from the nearest ocean. Another shop stocked merchandise from all around the world, specifically Europe, Asia, Africa, Mexico, and the USA (anything from Canada or South America be darned). Another had an area dedicated to headgear from around the world where they had cowboy hats, conical hats like the one Raiden wears, and of course sombreros in every possible size. They also had a hamburger hat to represent the United States because nothing says America quite like food-shaped accessories.

Had I been so inclined, I could have bought a fabulous Buddha doll, an Eagle talon backscratcher, a fake stuffed deer, a fake tiger skin rug, a trinket of a gecko holding a shotgun, an unimpressed Jesus statue, or a myriad of Christmas decorations (despite it being May). And I could have done it while listening to hard trance music blaring over the speakers, the singer periodically singing "Let me be your sex machine."

Among it all were more statues, both inside and outside every building I stepped into, of just about anything that had legs, including:

- A camel wearing a sombrero.
- A common turtle.
- A cow with a slot machine in its midsection.
- A hippo.
- A demonic lion with red eyes.
- A brontosaurus wearing a sombrero.
- A giant, red wiener dog.
- An alligator.
- A great white shark.
- A tiny whale.

And I took pictures of it all. I couldn't help myself. I had to capture what I saw to confirm I wasn't dreaming. If it had been a dream, Freud would have had a field day trying to explain the racist bizarro world I had imagined, but nope, this place was very real.

It was an unexpected reminder that there is still progress to be made in this country. My experiences thus far had been positive. I had met all kinds of people who were so different from me but also so much the same. Roland from Vermont had enjoyed my comedy; the waitress from Arkansas had helped me through a tough situation; the crowd in Florida had welcomed me despite my obvious differences. The United States was a wonderful place when it wasn't hating people for no reason.

That's what bothered me the most. South of the Border would have been a fun, quirky place if not for the offensive statues. Who wouldn't want to take a picture of a cow with a slot machine in its midsection? I just didn't understand why it had to be next to a piece of racist garbage.

I returned once again to my car. I had planned to spend just a few minutes on this side trip but was now nearing an hour in kitschy racistland, with nearly fifty pictures of what it offered. I started to question my decision.

Was I racist for having stayed and taken so many photos? Could I enjoy the pictures of the non-racist statues knowing where they had been taken? Why did this place exist in the first place? Did they know how insensitive it was? How much would it cost to buy my own T-rex statue? Was my journey to all fifty states better or worse for having decided to stop there?

I made my way back onto I-95 and into North Carolina. I knew that challenging myself to experience new things meant stepping outside of my comfort zone; I just assumed it would be for things like interacting more with strangers or sleeping in a car, not figuring how to react to a tourist trap driven by stereotypes.

I realized I needed this reminder. Not every detour was going to be perfect. For every Space and Rocket Museum, there was a South of the Border out there as well. And it was up to us to highlight the former and admonish the latter. Or at least poke fun of it with ridiculous photos.[41]

---

41 To see pictures from South of the Border, see tarv.in/southcarolina

15. PENNSYLVANIA

Standing Humble Brag
Philadelphia, PA. May 31, 2015

"I've been Andrew Tarvin. You all have been great, thank you."

It was a line I'd given hundreds of times before. I've said it at the end of talks at large conferences, the finish of hands-on trainings at companies, and once at the close of a coaching session when I forgot I was talking to just one other person.

But this time, the reaction to the line—or more likely my entire keynote   was a first.

I was checking off my eighth state in two weeks and had just finished my talk on humor for the closing day of the Association for Applied and Therapeutic Humor Conference in Philadelphia, Pennsylvania. Little by little, the audience rose to their feet, applauding.

I had received standing ovations from performances and as part of my workshops (though many of my workshops end on an exercise that leaves people standing, so when they applaud at the end of it, it's a standing ovation by default; no one has yet to sit down before clapping to make a point about it). But this—this was my first on-your-feet-clap as a response to my keynote.

As a speaker, there are few greater signs of a talk well spoken than a standing ovation. The best feedback is hearing from individuals about how you've positively helped them in some way. The second best is someone hiring you for another event because of what they saw, a sign that they believe others can benefit from your work (also $$$). The third, and most immediate sign is a standing ovation.

Applause is almost a mandatory response at this point, something we do for events we enjoy, when we want to give it up for all of the comedians we've seen tonight, or sarcastically when someone has messed up. A standing ovation means more. It's not required or expected. It's a handful of people saying, "I enjoyed this so much I'm willing to not be lazy for a moment and get out of my seat." And then everyone else behind them either agrees or decides to stand so they don't look callous in comparison.

And this was my first.

I looked at the smiling faces and took a deep breath to soak it all in. I was grateful, proud, and humbled all at the same time. I was grateful for the opportunity from the board of AATH to allow me to share my work. I was proud to have delivered a talk I was passionate about, the culmination of years of research, hard work, and formerly less-than-stellar-but-now-really-good talks at hundreds of organizations around the country. And I was humbled because the ovation came from a group of my peers—other people who apply humor in powerful ways, like therapy, medical care, research, academia, and in the corporate world like myself.

I had come a long way from my first speaking engagement, a hastily prepared talk in a conference room at Procter & Gamble in 2007. I had now delivered nearly 400 programs to more than 25,000 people around the world. I was more confident in my message, delivery, and wardrobe.

When I first started speaking, I suffered from imposter syndrome. What could people possibly learn from me, a nerdy engineer from Ohio with an affinity for puns and an obsession with efficiency?

I wouldn't say my life was served on a silver platter, but I also had things pretty good. My family didn't grow up the wealthiest, my parents divorced when I was a teenager, and I had to put myself through college. However, I didn't come from a poverty-stricken neighborhood, I'd never been systematically oppressed, and I had a pretty awesome mom.

In the United States, I am the majority: a straight white male. The only minority thing about me is that I'm left-handed, so I'll die seven years sooner and never be able to use right-handed scissors. Not bad compared to the challenges other people have to go through, including some of my peers on the AATH stage.

Peers like Beth Usher, the closing keynote of the conference, a woman, who at the age of seven, had to have half of her brain removed to stop an aggressive form of cancer and had to relearn how to do everything, and I mean everything, all over again. Or, Saranne Rothberg who survived stage IV cancer and turned her story and passion into a phenomenal nonprofit to help others in need. Or, countless others who have dedicated their decorated careers in helping others, like Allen Klein, Mary Kay Morrison, Chip Lutz, Karyn Buxman, Heidi Hanna, Julie Ann Sullivan, Barbara Grapstein, Joyce Saltman, and on and on and on.

I didn't have to overcome the same challenges they did, and I'll never fully know the privileges I've been afforded, but that didn't mean I didn't work hard to get to where I was. I got a scholarship for university because I worked hard in high school, and I got room and board paid for because I became an RA. I got the job at P&G because of my technical and business skills I had spent years developing and got the role in NYC because I had done well right out of school. I could create Humor That Works because I worked countless nights researching entrepreneurship, spent ten years working as a stand-up and improv comedian, and did hundreds of events to improve. And, I could live as a nomad because I created a flexible business, had built a network of friends and family across the country, and was foolish enough to ask, "Why not?"

I wasn't any different or any more special than anyone else, and that was the point. I don't consider myself an inspirational speaker, though I do hope to inspire; I consider myself an aspirational speaker. I want audiences to see me as someone who loves what they do, that uses humor to improve all aspects of work and life, and, most importantly, has had to learn how to do it. I want people to say, "If he can do it, surely I can as well." Because they can. You can. All it requires is making a choice.

And that's what I shared with AATH, a group of incredible people who have my same passion and enthusiasm for what humor can do. After the event, people told me incredible words of encouragement, a few gave me tips on how to improve, and many thanked me for the message I shared.

Speaking can be a stressful profession; it involves a lifetime of uncertainty and can often be a lonely endeavor. But it was moments like these that made it all worth it (that and the flexible schedule, exciting travel, solid compensation, diversity of clients, and brief moments of feeling like a rock star). I realized I didn't really care where I lived so long as I got to keep doing this for a living.

I stood on stage as the audience stood opposite me, and I bowed a thank you to the crowd. I thought about applauding all of them for letting me do what I love to do but realized it might look like I was applauding myself, and I'm not that narcissistic. My self-congratulations would come later, as I chowed down at Federal Donuts, a combo donut and fried chicken restaurant in South Philly. For the moment, I just enjoyed the attention, appreciating the appreciation.

Appreciation Scale

There are a lot of ways to show appreciation for someone else. Some of them are simple; others more involved. Some show how much you truly care; others, how much you barely do. To better understand how to appreciate someone in the future, refer to this handy list:

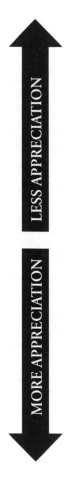

LESS APPRECIATION

MORE APPRECIATION

1. A smile.
2. Typing LOL.
3. A thumbs up.
4. Saying LOL.
5. A handshake.
6. Double thumbs up.
7. A high five.
8. Saying, "That's funny."
9. A fist bump.
10. Laughing.
11. Applauding.
12. A mention on social media.
13. A side hug.
14. Cheering.
15. A standing ovation.
16. A hug.
17. A testimonial.
18. A kiss.
19. A letter of reference.
20. A referral.
21. A LinkedIn recommendation.
22. Rebooking.
23. A heartful message explaining how you were impacted.
24. Money.

16. IOWA

The Vineyard Over the Hill
Stuart, IA. June 14, 2015

I finished taking my selfie and hopped in the car. I was with my brother, David, of "I want to trespass on private property for photoshopped dragon pictures" fame, and we were on our way to an open mic in Iowa. But we had seen a sign for a store called Drew's Quality Chocolates and had to stop for a selfie and some sweets.

It was Day One of our epic "Middle of the Country" road trip. After Philadelphia, I had gone back to Cincinnati for a day, then to Chicago and San Francisco for speaking engagements, and returned to Quad Cities, Illinois, for ComedySportz World Championships. From there I was going to drive through a few states until I got to Colorado for another speaking engagement.

David had the summer off from his lecturing duties at Texas A&M, so he decided to join me and the drive to Colorado turned into visiting twelve states in fourteen days. The first of which was Iowa, and all we needed was a place where I could perform before we drove to the next one.

After much Googling and phone calling, it appeared that a show at Dale Valley Winery at 15:00 in Stuart was the only place in the entire state that was having an open mic that day, so that's where we were headed.

We turned left out of My Quality Chocolates onto a two-lane road and made our way toward Stuart. As we entered the town, we passed a sign that read:

"Stuart, IA. Home to 1,700 Good Eggs (and a few stinkers)"

A town of 1,700 wasn't the smallest municipality I would perform in, but it was close. We continued our drive, reaching the single stop sign in town and made a right. As the "crowded streets" of downtown Stuart faded behind us, I wondered where in the "h-e-double hockey sticks" we were going.

"Where exactly are we going?" David asked, apparently thinking the same thing.

"To a winery. At least that's what the website said," I replied.

In less than a minute we were out of the town and on country roads. The afternoon sun revealed farmhouses, cows, and lots and lots of nothing. A few minutes passed as we drove on.

"What if it's just some dude's house?" I joked.

David laughed nervously, "I'm not sure if that would be funny or scary."

I agreed. The further we drove, the more country the roads got. The more country the roads got, the more nervous I was for what we were about to experience.

After five miles of nothing, we made a left onto an old road. It was an actual road but barely: no painted lines on the sides or down the middle, room for one and a half cars at a time. The possibility of it just being a dude's house seemed to be increasing. A mile later, Google told us to turn right onto a dirt road. We hesitated but continued.

I broke the tension in the car. "Umm . . . so if it's just a house, just turn around and book it. Some guy having an open mic at his home is either a serial killer or probably very handsy, and I'm not sure I want to deal with either of those things."

"Yeah, I was thinking the same thing," David replied as he eased the rental car along the dirt path.

We drove up a slight hill and saw a house on the left with a single car in the driveway. If that was the spot, there was no way we were staying. I started to tell David to nope right out of there but then noticed the No Trespassing sign and saw that the road continued beyond the hill.

We eclipsed the hill and the house, and both sighed with relief. Past the creepy No Trespassing place was a beautiful vineyard. There was a building on the left with an outdoor seating area and patio where fifteen or so people were gathered, listening to music. Rows of grapes, or whatever else you make wine with, grew behind the building. The dirt road led down into a parking lot where there were ten-plus cars already parked.

We drove down the hill and found a spot. As we walked up, we could hear "Ho Hey" ("I belong with you, you belong with me, you're my sweeth-eeeeaaaarrrrrrrt") by The Lumineers coming from the speakers. At first, I thought it was the radio—partly because it sounded so good and partly because I didn't think the people standing on stage would be the type to sing a The Lumineers song. I was wrong.

The performers were a duo. On electric bass rocked a tall, skinny guy with short brown hair and a goatee. On acoustic, and doing most of the vocals, was an older man who resembled George RR Martin but with braids and a driver cap. They didn't look like The Lumineers, but they did sound like them.

As the duo played, we approached a table with a piece of paper on it. Paper at an open mic usually indicates the sign-up list, and that's exactly what this happened to be. A man in his mid-forties sat at the sign-up table. He wore a black baseball cap down to his eyes and a crisp black t-shirt with no sleeves. He looked like what I imagined retired country stars looked like.

I introduced myself and said I was a comedian interested in doing the open mic. He flashed a smile and introduced himself as Bill. He, along with everyone we met there, was incredibly polite and welcoming. He put me on the sign-up list and told us to have a seat.

David went inside and got us some cheese, sausage, and crackers to munch on and a glass of wine.[42] I sat outside to go over my set list.

George RR Martin and friend finished their set and a solo artist got up to perform. With the built-in soundtrack of his music, I admired the scenery. The stage was set up under a newly built wooden shelter, the wood still bright and fresh. Ceiling fans created a light breeze with the summer air as music filled the surrounding area. Audience members sat at round, metal tables under the shelter and beyond. Rolling green hills and vibrant green trees surrounded the venue.

The solo artist finished his set, and Bill introduced me to the stage.

"And now, for a first here at the Dale Valley Winery, we have a comedian. Coming all the way from New York City, please welcome Drew Tarvin."

With that, I took the stage to scattered but enthusiastic applause. I talked about my nomadic journey, shared some jokes, and performed the "Clichéd Meaning of Life" poem.

I finished my set and received a warm round of applause. Various people came up to me afterward, some just to say I did great, others to ask for my card, and more than a few wanting to know if I had the poem on YouTube

42 The wine was a Marechal Foch they called Katydid, a three-year award-winning red with floral herbaceous notes and a smooth oak finish. It was so good David remembered the name of it immediately when I asked him what he drank.

somewhere. The owners of the venue told me I could come back whenever I wanted and that they were having a festival in a month if I'd like to perform in it. Bill and his wife offered to let us stay with them anytime we were back in town. And a couple of friendly couples gave recommendations for things to do on our upcoming journeys to Nebraska and Kansas.

The open mic had been an incredible start to our Middle of the Country road trip and served as a wonderful reminder of what the United States had to offer. In addition to the spacious skies and amber waves of grain, the United States had some fantastic humans. In less than an hour, our hesitation from turning onto that dirt road had passed, and we felt completely at home with the people of Stuart, Iowa. It was a positive lesson in not judging a book by its cover, a town by its size, or an open mic venue by its location behind a creepy house on a hill.

After a short break, the closing act of the afternoon stepped to the stage to perform, and they were the best of the evening. It was Bill and his band, the Mason Jars and the Gypsy Outlaws. I had no idea what the name meant, but I knew they were incredible performers and even nicer people.

17. NEBRASKA

I Am Not a Rapper
Omaha, NE. June 14, 2015

"I'm sorry, but that show was canceled by the producers," the hostess said. Her words said "I'm sorry," but her body language said, "I do not care at all about your situation."

I was in Omaha, Nebraska, at the Lookout Lounge. David and I were early for a poetry open mic that was supposed to start at "arguably Omaha's best small venue for music" in just over an hour. David was waiting in the car as I was trying to get details on the show. We had called at least ten times that day to confirm the event was still happening but never got an answer, so we showed up hoping the mic was still on. It was not.

This was less than ideal; you might even say it sucked. The day had started so well with the awesome trip to the Dale Valley Winery in Iowa followed by a short visit to the Heartland of America Park in downtown Omaha. Now, Lookout Lounge was ruining our best-laid plans.

We were only going to be in Nebraska for the evening before heading down to Kansas where I'd be speaking at Kansas State University the following morning. If I didn't perform in Omaha that night, we would have to backtrack during our carefully planned road trip, or I would have to skip checking Nebraska off my list.

I didn't want to do either, so I tried to brainstorm other options. I saw from the entrance of the lounge that there was something happening on stage. A sound resembling music with the bass turned up too loud came from the speakers, and a man gesticulated wildly to an audience of arm-waving people. I realized he was rapping.

I asked the hostess, "What show is going on right now?"

"It's a hip-hop show of a few local rappers," she unenthusiastically replied. I'm not 100 percent sure if she was smacking gum, but in my memory of the event now, she definitely was, and she smacked it annoyingly.

I paused for a second. "Could I perform on the show?"

"What?" she asked. Not in a "What? You're a rapper, that's so exciting you should definitely be able to get on," but more of a "What? Surely you cannot be serious right now."

I was surprised at my own response, but I was serious.[43] Because secretly, in high school, I dreamed of becoming an international hip-hop superstar. Yes, the same kid who lettered in bowling, played in the marching band, and was a mathlete, also wanted to rap. I wanted to impress with my lyrical flows that rose to the highs and lows of beats from a Bose.

And now, years later, I really wanted to perform while in Nebraska, and there was a hip-hop show just begging for me to be on it.

I tried again. "Could I perform? I'm a spoken word artist that's trying to perform in all fifty states. I was going to do the show later, but you said it's been canceled and now I won't get a chance to perform in your wonderful state of Nebraska."

She was not swayed by my Nebraska butt-kissery. She rolled her eyes. "Let me get the MC," she said as she walked away.

I wasn't sure if she meant MC as in the host or a rapper, but it didn't matter. My mind started racing about what I could say to the MC that would help me get on stage. I hadn't prepared any rhymes, but the "Clichéd Meaning of Life" poem was lyrical in a way and included a few hip-hop references. I could also improvise a rap based on a suggestion; it wouldn't be good, but it would be something.

I started rhyming words I saw around me to warm up just in case.

Door, floor, gimme some more.
The wall is tall, if I had a ball, I would fall, into a stall, at the mall.
Window . . . . . . window . . . .

"What's up?" a bearded man asked me, interrupting my sick mental rhymes. He was a few inches taller than me with a closely shaved head and an equally trimmed beard. His head reminded me of a tennis ball.

---

43 And don't call me Shirley. #Airplane!

Window . . . how you been though? Nailed it.

"Yo, what's up man?" I started with unintentional hip-hop slang in my voice. "I'm a performer trying to perform in all fifty states and was going to do the poetry show later tonight, but it got canceled, right? I do spoken word that's more like a capella rap and do improvised hip-hop. I was wondering if I could join your show, or even, you know, just do something real quick during a break or something."

The tennis ball looked at me in my J. Crew button-front checkered shirt, my hair styled into a mini-Conan O'Brien, and the nerdy expression that always sits on my countenance.

"Naw, man," and walked away.

I wanted to be mad at him, but I couldn't. If I was producing a show and some stranger came up halfway through it and asked to be on it, I would say no, too. Especially if that show was a hip-hop show and that stranger looked like me.

I wasn't going to fulfill my high school dreams that night, and we would have to find a way to get back to Nebraska after going to Kansas.[44] For a moment, I felt as if my childhood dream had been squashed once and for all. Perhaps this is what it meant to be an adult, letting go of your silly goals from adolescents in the face of real-world obstacles.

I walked outside to tell my brother the bad news.

"They canceled the show, I asked if I could flow, the dude said no, so we'll have to go."

David just looked at me.

Then again, I didn't have to rap on stage to keep the dream alive.

---

44 We would end up doing it the next day, adding 400 miles and nearly five hours to our trip, but successfully checking it off as a state.

The Aftermath Rap

I never truly gave up on my dream of being a rapper, as exhibited by this rap I wrote in 2009—when I was twenty-five years old.

Verse 1
So you think you're all cool, cuz u studied English,
Well I'm tired of stereotypes, so I'm 'bout to extinguish,
Any notions you had about a man of math
So listen up close, no repeats, simple paths.

Screw your fancy words, and use of synonyms,
I'm the top of the curve, while you a minimum.
Keep goin' parallel, and don't cross that line
Your life is trigged out, and you need a cosin.

Chorus
I go one one two, in the Fibonacci sequence,
Misbehave in class, cause juvenile delinquents.
So accept your fate, don't try to be a hero,
Cuz you just can't do it, like dividin' by zero.

Verse 2
Life is a numbers game, and it all adds up,
I'll divide you so bad, you'll wish for a pre-nup,
You 'bout to get subtracted from the situation,
Like simple math, you'll need an operation.

No matter what you say, we are not equals,
Cuz I'll always be there, and you'll be the sequel.
Like an arrow pointin' right, I'm greater than you
A smooth operator, I'm g-r-eight-times-two.

Chorus
I go one one two, in the Fibonacci sequence,
Misbehave in class, cause juvenile delinquents.
So accept your fate, don't try to be a hero,
Cuz you just can't do it, like dividin' by zero.

Verse 3
My rhymes is calculated, it's true I won't lie,
But merckin you fools is as easy Pi.
I'm three point one four, one five nine,
No decimal repeats, cuz I'm one of a kind.

Are you frightened now? I know that I'm scary
But unlike the little i, I ain't imaginary.
But I've made my point, just like a decimal,
You're just too small, you're infinitesimal.

Now I hope you understand, after hearin' my wrath
There ain't nothin' left, except this aftermath.

Chorus
I go one one two, in the Fibonacci sequence,
Misbehave in class, cause juvenile delinquents.
So accept your fate, don't try to be a hero,
Cuz you just can't do it, like dividin' by zero.

18. KANSAS

Gassed
Somewhere in Kansas. June 14, 2015

We drove south on US-75 on our way to Topeka. David was nodding off in the passenger seat as I powered through. It was late, we were both tired, and it had been a long day. The rain outside had turned into a light sprinkle as we drove through the night. A James Patterson audiobook played through the speakers.

I looked down at the gas tank and noticed it was heading toward empty. I clicked through the menu on the dash and found the estimated miles remaining sat at just above sixty. I saw lights up ahead and asked David to look on Google for gas stations.

After the moment of confusion that comes from being awakened suddenly, he did some tapping on his phone. "If you turn left coming up, there's a gas station ten miles that way. Or there should be some along this road in thirty miles or so."

Turning left meant adding at least twenty miles to the trip and forcing us to backtrack, something I hated doing. I think there's something about having to turn around that says, "I didn't do this as efficiently as I could have," or perhaps even more egregious, "I was wrong."

It's like when you're walking somewhere and you realize you forgot something. You have that awkward moment where you know you have to turn around, but instead of just doing a 180, you take out your phone and pretend you just got a message that is changing where you're headed. Or you just go around the block the long way to prevent the obvious U-turn.[45]

Not one to backtrack, I said, "We'll get the ones in thirty miles."

David went back to sleep, and I drove along, the clock ticking past midnight in the Kansas dark.

Thirty or so miles later we came upon the first gas station. I had almost missed it because all of the lights were off; it was closed. I continued down the street. The next gas station had a few lights on near the pumps, so I slowed down and started to turn in before seeing the darkened windows of the station building; it too was closed. I pressed on.

David stirred awake.

"Uh, can you check any of the times for the gas stations?" I asked.

David thumbed away at his phone as I continued along. Two more gas stations, both closed.

"Most of them don't say, but the one we just passed closed at midnight," David answered.

Neither of us had stopped to think that gas stations in the middle of Kansas might not all be open 24/7. I thought this was America. Shouldn't I have the freedom to buy those white powdered sugar donuts at any time of night? Perhaps I'd been living in NYC for too long.

I checked the estimated miles remaining. It had dropped to twenty; the car either wasn't very good at predicting or I had driven too fast to be gas efficient. "Can you see where the nearest one is that is definitely open?"

"Well," David replied, "there's the one back the way we came, about forty miles away. Or there's one near Topeka, twenty-five miles away."

If the car was to be believed, both were too far to reach with our current fuel level. I pulled over to the side of the road and turned off the Patterson book.

"We don't have enough gas to get to either of those places," I said.

We both thought for a moment.

"We could sleep here for a bit and then get gas in the morning," David offered.

It was certainly better than trying to make it somewhere and running out of gas more in the middle of nowhere than we already were. At least there were buildings here, and the gas stations would open eventually. Though buildings also meant there were places for murderers to hide. Maybe we weren't as safe as I had assumed.

I considered the possibility that I had made a mistake in not getting gas

---

45 The one exception to this is a revolving door. Revolving doors are the best method of entering a building because if, while heading through the door, you realize it's the wrong building, you can just continue revolving around until you're back outside. No awkward U-turn at all. Also, they're supposedly more energy efficient or something.

earlier. Was I foolish for not wanting to go ten miles in the wrong direction just to fuel up and then retrace those ten miles to get back on track? Would I have to admit my desire for efficiency had doomed us to a night spent in the car? I remembered my experience in the Walmart parking lot and cringed at the thought of sleeping in the car again, especially since this time I'd have a roommate.

There had to be another way—or at least a way that made our predicament not my fault. I reasoned that if anyone were to blame, it was probably David. He had told me there were gas stations thirty miles away. How was I to know they would be closed? Then again, how was he? I argued both sides in my head for a moment before David in my head was interrupted by David in the car.

"What do you want to do?" he asked.

I was about to start blaming David in the car when a thought struck me.

"I wonder . . ." I said aloud, talking more to myself than him.

I turned the car around and headed back to the second gas station I had seen, the one with lights on at the pump but that was still closed.

"What are you doing?" David asked.

"I wonder if the pumps are still on. The lights are on so maybe that means the pumps are on."

I checked the little arrow next to the gas pump icon on the dash to confirm which side the tank was on and pulled into the station. The pumps were well lit, but the building was completely dark. A neon Bud Light sign in the station window was distinctly off. If this were a horror film, there would most definitely be a mass murderer waiting inside.

But the lights on the pump gave me hope. I inserted my credit card and removed it. I entered my zip code and waited. Well, to be honest, I started to enter my zip code but hit the wrong number, so I hit clear thinking that it would just erase the last digit, but instead, it wiped the whole screen. So, I repeated the process, entered my zip code correctly, and then waited.

"Please select grade and begin fueling" the digital screen read.

I almost jumped for joy but reserved my emotions. It still might not work. I may still have to blame David. I went to open the gas cap, but it had no nub, so I returned to the other side of the car and opened the driver's side door to find the lever to pop it open. I looked near the floor. Nope. I looked near the center. Nope. I looked on the door itself. Nope. This was the problem with always driving rental cars: you never knew how to open the gas cap or pop the trunk.

"What are you doing?" David asked.

"I'm looking for how you open the gas cap thingy."

"You just push on it."

I knew that. (I didn't know that.) I walked back around, pushed the lid open and unscrewed the cap. I pressed the lowest grade—because who doesn't—and inserted the nozzle. I squeezed the handle, and after a brief second, I could hear gas flowing into the tank.

It worked! Annoyingly, the little metal piece you used to keep the handle pressed without having to hold it was broken, but the gas worked! I filled the tank, screwed the cap on, put everything away, and closed the lid. I sat back down in the car.

"I can't believe that worked," I admitted.

David replied, "I can't, either. Is it supposed to?"

"I have no idea," I said as I pulled back onto the road. I had saved the night; we could continue onto Topeka and sleep in actual beds. In the morning, I'd deliver a great event at Kansas State University, and we'd celebrate by getting delicious ice cream from Call Hall Dairy Bar, K-State's very own creamery. Best of all, I didn't have to blame my brother or admit I was wrong.

"You're welcome," I accidentally said aloud.

"What?" David asked.

"Nothing."

19. OKLAHOMA

The Love of Performance
Oklahoma City, OK. June 16, 2015

Every single night, all across the country, there are artists pouring their hearts and souls into a performance. Some sing songs, others recite poetry, and more than a few rap their thoughts. And hardly anyone is watching them.

When we think of performance, we often think of the large-scale productions we're used to seeing: the stadium-sized concerts from platinum-selling artists, the packed comedy shows from TV-credentialed comedians, and sold-out runs from Broadway performers who were, at one time or another, on the show *Glee*.

But before a performer ever gets to that place, they do shows in the basements of bars, the back rooms of churches, and anywhere they can put together a makeshift stage. Performing for 500 is much easier than performing for five, but it's the five-person shows that mold you as an artist. It's in those performances that you get to see the true passion of an actor, comedian, or musician.

And that's what David and I were witnessing as we watched a play from the sidelines, above an outdoor theater on an ordinary sidewalk. We were in the Myriad Botanical Gardens in Oklahoma City, Oklahoma. After our gas scare and subsequent trip to Kansas State, we had driven back to Nebraska for a show and then back through Kansas to Oklahoma for a show, dinner, and a walk in the park.

The play we were watching was Shakespeare's *The Winter's Tale*, and the general vibe was "whelp" (with a shoulder shrug). The performance was part of the summer Shakespeare in the Park series, and the actors were giving it all they had despite the small turnout.

In fact, if you looked solely at the actors, you would have no idea they were performing for only a handful of people. They were decked out in full period garb, makeup exaggerating their features so they could be seen from the back of the theater. They spoke from their diaphragm as if they were in front of a sold-out crowd on a Broadway stage in New York City.

However, if you looked solely at the audience, you would have no idea they were watching a Shakespearean play, or anything at all. The outdoor theater could seat more than a hundred patrons, but the sparse collection of roughly ten people was scattered about as if the other ninety were never going to show up. The only difference between this audience and a group of complete strangers randomly sitting outside was that they all happened to be facing the same direction and only a few were talking.

I sympathized with the actors; I had certainly been there. About thirty minutes ago, in fact. Prior to coming to the park, David and I were at a music open mic in the downtown area. It was the only show I could find during our time in Oklahoma, and I needed it for the performance. It didn't matter that it was only for a family of four and three musicians just waiting for their turn to perform.

It wasn't the worst show of my journey—that honor belonged to West Virginia—but it was one of the smallest. The audience had been polite but was clearly waiting for music and not jokes. I still gave it all I could, just as these thespians were doing in the park.

The performers I respected the most were the ones who committed no matter the circumstances. As they teach at The Second City, a small crowd is no excuse to phone it in. For those people in the audience, it might be their only opportunity to see you perform. Or maybe they had made sacrifices to see the show: they had hired a babysitter or traveled in from miles away. I mean this probably wasn't true for this play in the park or the open mic earlier, but still.

The reality is that if those few never showed up, you wouldn't have anyone to perform for at all. Doing stand-up without an audience is just you talking to yourself in one-liners and puns. It's why I'm always grateful for anyone who comes to one of my shows or attends one of my events—without them I'm no different than Tom Hanks in *Cast Away*.

And whether the audience is one or one thousand, the art still matters. A music open mic in a pizza cafe can still inspire a little girl in the audience to learn guitar. A comedy show in a basement can still help a stressed-out young professional get over a recent breakup. A play in a park can still remind observers of the power and importance of art.

I remembered the first time I truly understood that truth. It was when I opened for a comedian named Steve Trevino at a Funny Bone in Huntington, West Virginia, back in 2007. He was a gracious headliner, and his material was as dirty as it was hilarious. After our second show of the weekend, a couple came up to us—well mostly him—and thanked him profusely. I wondered why they were so grateful Steve had shared some sex jokes with them when I heard the woman say, "Our best friend passed away last week, and this was the first time we've been able to laugh. So thank you."

Art and performance have this incredible power to transform a moment, provide catharsis, shift perspective, or bring you closer together with another human being. And you never know when someone who wants or needs those things might be in your audience. For the performers who truly respect their craft and the audiences who are willing to come witness it, every performance means something.

I had the opportunity to see performers with that level of commitment throughout my travels—from the Mason Jars and Gypsy Outlaws in Stuart to African-American Shakespear in Pensacola to Jose Hernandez, the singer-songwriter we had heard earlier that day in OKC. Even the amateur wrestlers I would see in Minneapolis were inspiring. The match pitted a guy with a beard and no shirt versus a guy with a shirt but no beard. Beard guy won, and it made me happy.

Those passionate performers giving it their all were always the most compelling to watch. They weren't always the best; in fact, sometimes they were the worst, but they were the most inspiring. It wasn't something I had been looking for when I started my journey, but the small shows in small venues in small towns were quickly becoming one of my favorite parts of the trip.

David and I watched the OK presentation of *The Winter's Tale* a while longer before we finally exited, not pursued by a bear.

20. NEW MEXICO

Adventure in New Mexico
Cochiti Pueblo, NM. June 17, 2015

The rain started lightly at first, a welcome respite from the summer heat. In a short while, we would reach the top of the hike, where we would see incredible views of the surrounding canyons and tent rock, formed from volcanic explosions millions of years ago. We would pass deep green bushes, vibrant cactus flowers, and barren trees. There would be a boulder you could jump from to make it look like you were flying high above the New Mexican plains.

But for the moment, we were surrounded by white rock, the walls on either side of us sanded down from years of weathering and erosion. David and I were hiking in Kasha Katuwe Tent Rocks near Santa Fe, New Mexico. After our stop in the park in OKC, we had made our way to Amarillo, Texas and crashed for the night. When we awoke in the morning, we stopped at Cadillac Ranch and then made our way toward Santa Fe, stopping at these Tent Rocks on the way.

As we snaked our way through the slot canyon, the drizzle became drops and soon reached a downpour. David and I ducked under an overhanging rock to escape the increasing precipitation, the rain reaching torrential quickly. The weather had gone from "not a cloud in the sky" to "very much some clouds in the sky, specifically the kind that hold water," in a matter of minutes.

Rain in a slot canyon is always dangerous, as it can lead to flash floods and strong currents that can knock you against the walls or sweep you under rocks. Based on our expert meteorology skills and general ignorance to the dangers of such situations, we assumed the rain would dissipate as quickly as it came, and that all we had to do was wait. Luckily we were right.

We took the moment to take a break. I grabbed our water bottles from my bag and handed David his. I also pulled out a protein bar and bit in. Rain turned the white rock around us into slippery brown walls, and a breeze swept through the canyon. We sat quietly, either out of awe of our environment or because we had run out of things to say after the 1,100 miles we had already driven in the car together.

I was reminded of our adventures from when we were kids. When I was growing up, adventuring was a family activity. We'd go on fun hikes where my oldest brother Adam would jump and climb around, and I'd rat on him, saying "Mom, look what Adam's giving me bad ideas about."

During our summer months, David and I would explore the wilderness of our suburban neighborhood, finding newts and snakes to let loose in our basement accidentally. We'd wander around the undeveloped parts of our subdivision as we wondered what it was like to be an explorer from years ago. We imagined ourselves as Lewis and Clark, Martin and Osa Johnson, or Chip and Dale (rescue rangers, not actual Chippendales).

We used to come up with elaborate backstories about our adventures. "Alright, so we're two famous adventurers who survived a plane crash in the jungle and home is our fort, but the neighborhood pool is a crocodile-infested river we have to swim across. Also, there are probably dinosaurs." There were almost always dinosaurs in our adventures; we weren't ones for historical accuracy.

And here we were again, twenty years later, still exploring. The only difference was our Hi-Cs were replaced with waters, our granola bars had become protein bars, and our neighborhood was replaced with the larger world around us.

I turned to David. "Remember when . . ."

". . . we used to hike like this as kids?" he automatically filled in.

"Yeah," I replied.

"Yeah," he replied.

It was one of the most meaningful conversations of our entire trip. That's not to say we didn't have other great conversations; it was just that at that moment we were both transported back in time to a period when we had no worries. We weren't concerned about bills, we didn't think about having to eat healthily, and we had no jobs to stress us out. Our biggest concern was what our next adventure was going to be and who got to be Chip and who had to be Dale.

Some might say we were reliving our childhood, but that's a sad notion to me. Why must exploring and using your imagination be something only children do? We weren't reliving our childhood but rather living our now-hood.

It's why I still considered myself an adventurer. I still liked to do unusual and exciting experiences or activities, and that's the dictionary definition of the word (plus I owned a headlamp). So what if on most days David taught public speaking and intercultural communication at a university and that in a few days I'd be training a group of senior executives how to communicate more effectively? For the moment, we were exploring an unknown (to us) land and fulfilling one of the reasons I loved to travel.

A few minutes later, the rain subsided. I finished my protein bar and put the wrapper in my bag (carry in, carry out). I took another drink of water and put both of our water bottles away. I took the lead as we hiked our way up toward the top of the canyon where beautiful views were waiting.

I turned to David, "Alright, we're two famous, and incredibly handsome, adventurers . . ."

21. COLORADO

Earning the View
Outside Colorado Springs, CO. June 19, 2015

Based purely on the name, where would you rather go: Garden of the Gods or Pikes Peak?

If you know nothing of the two parks in Colorado, the answer is easy: Garden of the Gods. It clearly has a cooler name. It sounds majestic, epic, and grandiose. Pikes Peak sounds like the highest point at someone's house.

The truth is Pikes Peak is better than Garden of the Gods. Don't get me wrong; Garden of the Gods is a beautiful place, filled with impressive red and white rocks jutting from the Earth, with beautiful hiking trails and great routes for the outdoorsy rock climbers who know how to belay. But the best part about it is the branding.

Within the Garden of the Gods you'll find: Cathedral Spires, Keyhole Window, Kissing Camels, Sleeping Giant, and Tower of Babel. These are all just different names for really big rocks.

Pikes Peak, however, is an experience, an experience that David and I were about to, well, experience.

We had just gotten through the toll at the entrance of Pikes Peak and were pulled over to the side of the road. David, my brother and fearer of heights, decided he didn't want to drive the nineteen-mile stretch of road to the summit. He had driven most of the way from Santa Fe, and I had no such fear of heights.[46]

We buckled up and started our ascent to the top. The drive started simple enough. A wide road traversed through aspen trees on a gradual incline. We passed picnic areas, hiking trails, and a Big Foot Crossing sign we stopped for a picture with. But as we climbed, the road got windier, narrower, and more "we might fall off this mountain-ier."

About halfway through the drive, we hit a series of switchbacks that I took slower than I wanted but faster than I should have. The tires of our Chevy Malibu rental car clung to the road for dear life as we rounded each corner, mere inches from a precipitous drop into mountainy doom. David grabbed the "Oh no" handle and didn't let go for the remainder of the drive.

Along the way, we saw a few viewpoints we considered stopping at but elected to push forward. We were in early and wanted to beat the long line of cars behind us to the top. Plus, I've learned that if you're doing any type of out-and-back, it's generally better to get to the top first and then take pictures on the way down. Often the views you thought were great will get trumped by better views as you climb higher, plus taking pictures gives you an excuse to rest on the second half of the trip.

As we pressed upward, the view around us went from green trees to brown rock to white snow in a matter of miles. We made it to the top without incident but with much stress and guessed at a parking space in the snow-covered lot. We headed to the edge and stopped to take in the beauty that we saw.

They say on a clear day you can see five different states from what is nearly the middle of Colorado when standing at the top of Pikes Peak. I don't know if that's true, but I do know that on any given day you can see a combination of inspiration and perspective on the beauty that is this planet.

I looked up and saw nothing but a gradient of blue sky as the cool breeze of standing 14,000 feet above sea level aggressively caressed my face. I looked straight out and saw snowcapped mountains in the distance and the slight curve of the horizon on our spherical planet. I looked down and found more sky with scattered pockets of visible liquid droplets and frozen crystals because, holy wow, we were higher than the clouds.

Past the sky, the beauty continued onward and outward with the green trees of aspen forests and the rocky ridges of the Rocky Mountain Trail. I took a deep breath of the thinner air as I admired the view; Kanye West's "Touch the Sky" played in my head.

---

46 I reserved my phobias for things that were truly scary, like how one day I might die by sneezing. Not that the sneeze itself will kill me, but that I'll be driving along and will let out a powerful sneeze that will cause my head to whip forward, smashing against the steering wheel causing me to veer off the road into a ravine. On second thought, maybe I shouldn't have agreed to drive.

For a moment, I forgot about all of the people standing around me, including David, and soaked it all in. A single tear dropped from my eye, not because of how beautiful the view was, but because the wind was something fierce atop the mountain, and I have sensitive eyes.

This was Pikes Peak. Part of me appreciated the simplicity of the name. In our overbranded world, it was refreshing not to be bombarded by hyperbole or unsubstantiated claims, like how I performed at a "World Famous" bar in Charleston, West Virginia. What makes it world famous? The owner's cousin who lives in Canada has heard of it? Am I world famous because someone from Russia left a comment on one of my YouTube videos telling me I suck? And why stop at the world? I saw a pair of socks in a Walmart that claimed they were the universe's coziest socks. If you're going to claim Earth, you might as well claim Milky Way galaxy because we can't say for sure.

Pikes Peak was simple. And yet part of me wished it was called something cooler, like the Precipice of Unicorns. Something that actually compelled people to step away from their Instagram accounts and actually see the world around them.

Before long, the first gondola of the morning arrived and the area flooded with people, snapping me out of my nature trance. I felt like Bill Bryson in *A Walk in the Woods*. I resented the tourists because they took the easy way up despite literally just thinking that more people should see this view.

I mean, at least David and I had earned our spot! Not like the people we saw hiking the mountain as we drove up in our air-conditioned and then later heated car, listening to music and sipping chocolate milk. We weren't hikers, but our harrowing drive made us more worthy than someone just stepping into a room strapped to a cable.

We milled about a bit longer before checking out the gift shop that sits atop the mountain. Nothing says, "I love nature," quite like being able to buy a sweatshirt that says exactly that while standing on top of said nature.

David asked if I wanted a souvenir to commemorate our trip. I declined. I'd rather collect stories and pictures than knick-knacks and paddy-whacks because, the reality is, nothing in that gift shop could exceed the gift you get from the view just outside the building, not even the overpriced and underdelicious donuts of the Pikes Peak Summit House. Besides, I was living out of two carry-on bags; where would I put it?

We headed back to the car. I started toward the driver's seat, but David said he'd drive. I think the one thing he feared more than driving near the edge of near certain doom was being in the passenger seat when I was doing it.

We got in the car and made our way down. As he drove, I calmly grabbed hold of the "Oh no" handle and prayed to the Garden of the Gods.

Improved Park Names

To improve the marketing of a few places to put them on par with Garden of the Gods, I renamed the following parks:

OLD PARK NAME	NEW PARK NAME
Pikes Peak	Precipice of Unicorns
Yellowstone	Mother Nature's Golden Palace
Grand Canyon	Grand Fissure of the Planets
Arches	God's Playdough
Olympic	Triumvirate of Worldly Domains
Glacier	Fortification of Frozen Water
Great Smoky Mountains	Stairway to the Clouds
Zion	Hanging Valleys of Zion
Acadia	Dawn of American Beauty
Grand Teton	Throne of Athena
Mammoth Cave	Lidenbrock's Labyrinth
Yosemite	Menagerie of Looney Tunes
Bryce Canyon	Odin's Cathedral
Sequoia	Origins of Eriador
Redwood	Forest of Crimson Timber
Everglades	Eternal Armory of Alligators

IDAHO

Exploring the Caves in Idaho
Arco, ID. June 21, 2015

I found myself standing in the dark, the only light coming from the hole I had just climbed through. A cool breeze kissed my face as the sound of dripping water blopped in my ear. *Blop.*

I was at the awesomely named Craters of the Moon Park in Arco, Idaho, with David. After hitting up Colorado, we made our way through Wyoming and Utah before stopping at the park on our way to Pocatello. Side note: Pocatello is the western version of Tuscáloosa in that it's just a fun city to say.

The Idahomer National Monument with the sweet name consisted of a vast ocean of lava flows, created from volcanic eruptions occurring thousands of years ago. According to TripAdvisor reviews, the park included "fascinating landscapes" that "look like the lunar surface."[47] It also included lava tube caves that David and I wanted to explore.

A half an hour earlier, my brother and I were standing in the Welcome Center talking to one of the rangers. Now I was standing in a cave in the dark, thinking about what she had said.

"Have either of you been in a cave, east of the Rocky Mountains, since 2005?" the ranger asked.

It was quite the question. First, I had to remember what all I've done in the last ten years, and second, I had to visualize all the places east of the Rocky

---

47 This last description was not written by Neil Armstrong, so it's hard to confirm its accuracy.

Mountains.

I had no clue. The last cave I remembered being in was the terrifying Mushroom Mines near Morehead, Kentucky, but I had no idea how long ago that was. At least five years ago, maybe fifteen.

"We're not sure." My brother and I responded. Well, he responded, and I nodded.

"Well, are you wearing anything that you might have worn when you were last in a cave?" she continued.

"Oh, no," we both said. I do have clothes I still fit into from five years ago (heck I still have clothes I fit into from twenty years ago), but I hadn't brought any of them with me, not even my middle school Future Class of 2002 shirt.

"Why do you ask?" I continued.

"We're trying to prevent the spread of a fungus that can kill bats."[48]

"Okay, thanks."

Thirty minutes later, while standing in a dark cave, it finally sank in. If we can't wear the same clothes because fungus might kill the bats, that means there are bats at Craters of the Moon. Bats live in caves—I'm in a cave. Holy crap, I'm in a cave with bats (maybe).

I glanced around into the nothingness in front of me. Who knows what possibly lay before me in the darkness of my environment? I felt an unexpected squeezing around my head. I wondered if this is what it felt like before fainting from fear. Then I remembered the squeezing was due to the headlamp I was wearing.

That's right, I had a headlamp. It was one of the few things I schlepped around the country with me, along with:

- Clothing: shirts, jeans, workout clothes, underwear, socks, a suit, a light raincoat, a winter coat, gym shoes, dress shoes, boots, sandals, and a hoodie for every day of the week.[49]
- Technology: my phone, laptop, iPod, a GoPro, an audio recorder, dongles, big headphones, little headphones, and eight thousand charging cables.
- Tools: my Titanium spork, a rubber clothesline, inflatable hangers, and a headlamp.

In total, it was thirty-nine pounds' worth of clothing, gear, and Pop

---

48 Something I later learned was called White Nose Syndrome (WNS), a fungus that was responsible for the death of hundreds of thousands of bats in eastern US caves. It turns out Batman's greatest foe wasn't the Joker but spores.

49 That's not to say I had seven different hoodies; I just wore the same hoodie every single day.

Tarts. And, of all the items I had, it was the eighty-five grams of headlamp that I was given the most sass for. As my friend Tamara claimed, "What could you possibly need a headlamp for? You're not going spelunking, and you're not roughing it out in nature. Everywhere you go, you'll have electricity."

Well, take that, Tamara. It had taken more than three months of travel, but I was finally about to justify why I carried this light on a headband as one of my few possessions, and it was going to save me from death by bat.

I pressed into the moundy nub to turn the light on but instinctively closed my eyes as it happened. I knew I wanted illumination; I just wasn't sure if I wanted to see what it revealed.

I opened my eyes slowly and was surprised by what I found before me. To my left was rock. On the right, both high and low was rock. And directly in front me, just a foot away, was rock. I was in a very small cave. Like shockingly small.

I had assumed from the darkness that the cave was massive, the size of the Glittering Caves from *Lord of the Rings* or the grotto in *The Goonies*. Instead, it was roughly the size of a phone booth. The wind had come from a small hole in the cave above my head. The water dripping was six inches to my right. There were no bats.

I shimmied my way out of the hole to return to the outside where my brother was standing.

"How was it?" David asked.

"Well, I guess it's technically a cave in the same way that watermelon is technically a berry, but, like, come on. It might be better to move to next one."

And we did. In total, we visited four more caves that day: Buffalo Cave, Beauty Cave, Boy Scout Cave, and Indian Tunnel. We saw massive underground openings, impressive stone structures, and lots and lots of rock. At no point did we see any bats, Louisville Slugger or otherwise.

But, in every single cave, I used my headlamp. Granted I didn't need to in one of the caves, but I wanted to make shadow puppets on the wall. My careful planning 180 days earlier had paid off, affording us the opportunity to have light during a dark time (I mean this only literally).

And that's sometimes how preparation works. You invest early on but don't see the fruits of that labor until much later, like in farming, 401Ks, and buying Hamilton tickets.

Some might ask: was it worth carrying the headlamp around only to use it for one day? Others might inquire: couldn't you have just bought a headlamp when you knew you were going to visit caves? A few might wonder: why not just use the flashlight on your smartphone? To those people I say, "Absolutely," "Maybe," and "Shut up."

Sometimes it's better to be overprepared than underprepared. Sometimes just knowing you have the right tools can be comforting, even if you never actually use them. Sometimes, you'll do anything to justify a decision you made so you don't have to admit someone else might be right.

Besides, without my headlamp, I might still be lost in the dark in Idaho.

23. MONTANA

I'm Getting Fat
Bozeman, MT. June 22, 2015

I've always been skinny. I was born 8.3 pounds and stayed that way until I was fifteen years old. By the time I entered college, I stood 5'11" and weighed a whopping 130 pounds. After a year of working out five days a week and eating as much food as I could, I bumped up to a massive 140. I hovered around that number until I started my travels.

What was my secret? A strict diet and exercise regimen—just kidding. Genetics, a high metabolism, and always being active. It most certainly wasn't from eating healthy.

I learned early on I could eat pretty much anything I wanted and not gain weight, so I took advantage of that. The way I saw it, eating junk food and not gaining weight was my superpower. If I ate foods like salad and quinoa instead of delicacies like Twinkies and Ho-Hos, I was wasting that superpower. It would be like if Clark Kent wasn't Superman, just a mediocre reporter at the Daily Planet.

But that was changing. Four months into my journey, I was statistically the fattest I'd ever been.[50] And I knew why: I was pregnant, and the father was food.

Because when you travel, you want to ingest the best of what the locale

---

50 I know this because I periodically take health measurements, including, at the time, weight (151 pounds), stomach size (32.75"), biceps (12.5"), blood pressure (103/63), cholesterol (157 mg/dL), and sense of ego (overinflated).

has to offer. No one wants to eat the "Best Kale in All of Wyoming." No, if you go to Wyoming, you get a Bison Burger. If you go to Colorado, you try the Rattlesnake/Pheasant hot dog. In Massachusetts, you get a frappe. In Rhode Island, you drink a cabinet. In New York, you get pizza (thin crust). In Chicago, you get pizza (thick crust). In St. Louis, you get pizza (cardboard).

And when you're in Bozeman, Montana, you go to La Parrilla, a "casual quick-service fusion grill with a Mexican flare." And that's where David and I found ourselves. After exploring the caves at Craters of the Moon and delivering an event at Idaho State University, we had made our way into Montana, first to Helena and then to Bozeman for a show. But before the jokes we needed food, and Foursquare recommended La Parrilla. We checked out their site and were sold:

> *La Parrilla (or La Pa as it is affectionately known) is a burrito shop that has been a favorite part of the quintessential Bozeman food experience since 1996. Fresh, high-quality food is grilled and prepared before your eyes, blending bold flavors from around the world. Burritos, tacos, bowls, and salads are artfully created and personalized for each guest by an eclectic, boisterous, funny (but hey, looks aren't everything) staff. La Pa puts the whole world in your hands.*

They put the whole world in your hands; David and I couldn't help but go there.

At first glance, the restaurant seemed like every other quick-service Mexican joint. They had boldly colored walls, fiesta-inspired decor, and multicolored signage. Their logo was written in a "fun" font, and the burritos came wrapped in foil and placed in the plastic vented baskets that seem to exist solely for burritos. And that's where the similarities ended.

The staff behind the counter was, as described, boisterous and funny, and actually seemed to enjoy their jobs, something not often seen at Taco Bell, Del Taco, Taco Taco Taco, or Let's Taco Bout It. And, unlike some of those other restaurants, this place was jumping despite the fact that it wasn't 2 a.m., and the clientele wasn't drunk.

But the real differentiator was the menu with their selection of World Fusion Burritos, what they had self-described as the blending of bold flavors from around the world. And a blend they were. There was the *Bombay Bomburrito* that included ginger banana chutney with cabbage and green curry sauce, or the *Buffalo Gypsy* with organic bison, spicy bean spread, and Chinese BBQ sauce. Not feeling any of those? You could also get a *Blackwater Bayou, Bourbon BBQ,* or the excellently named *Wrap of Khan.*

Despite the twenty-plus options available for feasting, I immediately knew what I wanted upon setting my eyes on their colorfully written menu. The creative mad scientists at La Pa had created the Holy Grail of cylindrical food: the Chicken Fettuccini Alfredo Burrito.

The gluttonous wrap was exactly as it sounds: a marvel of innovation, consisting of Fettuccine noodles smothered in a rich Alfredo sauce with pieces of grilled chicken, all wrapped in a flour tortilla. Because when you're looking to fill a burrito with something, you find the heaviest food you can.

I excitedly ordered the masterpiece, paid, and took the massive pasta wrap to my seat. I unwrapped the foil just enough to expose the top—I've learned my lessons from Chipotle—and took a bite. My mouth exploded with the deliciousness of pasta, protein, sauce, and tortilla coming together to flood my taste buds with flavor. It was like having an Italian chef doing the merengue on my tongue, singing "That's Amore."

I continued chowing down on the miracle food, stopping only long enough to congratulate myself for a well-placed order and to take a picture.[51]

This was the American dream. When our forefathers worked to create a new republic for which we stand and promised us life, liberty, and the pursuit of happiness, they surely meant the ability to eat Chicken Fettuccine Alfredo in a burrito. It was everything that was beautiful about this country. It was innovative: a unique combination of two existing ideas filling an unarticulated need I never knew I had. It was diverse: a pristine example of two cultures working together to build something incredible. And it was gluttonous: a 1,000-plus calorie meal that laughed in the face of the recommended daily calorie count. In short, it was America.

I finished the entire thing because I'm a champion. I felt uncomfortably full but comfortably okay with that, and I understood why the staff here was so happy. Every day, they got a chance to serve up a little bit of the US of A to whoever walked in.

I leaned back in my wooden chair, slyly unbuttoned the button on my jeans to allow more room for stomach, and promptly slipped into a food coma. Sure, I was a little bit fatter, but I was a lotta bit happier.

---

51 See the picture at tarv.in/montana

My Favorite Food Spot in Each State

If you're looking for something healthy to eat in each state, pick up *The Boring Way to Eat: A Guide to America's Best Salads.* If you're looking for the most delicious thing to eat, check out these places.

Alabama	*Lambert's Cafe*	**Montana**	*La Parilla*
Alaska	*The Hot Bite*	**Nebraska**	*Crescent Moon Café*
Arizona	*Picazzo's*	**Nevada**	*Mon Ami Gabi*
Arkansas	*The Afterthought*	**New Hampshire**	*Red Arrow Diner*
California	*In N Out*	**New Jersey**	*Windmill Hot Dogs*
Colorado	*Biker Jim' Dogs*	**New Mexico**	*La Choza*
Connecticut	*Whole Donut*	**New York**	*Original Shake Shack*
Delaware	*The Charcoal Pit*	**North Carolina**	*Sutton's Drug Store*
Florida	*Bristol's Burger*	**North Dakota**	*Sandy's Donuts*
Georgia	*Leopold's Ice Cream*	**Ohio**	*Graeter's Ice Cream*
Hawaii	*Kua'aina Sandwich*	**Oklahoma**	*Sauced*
Idaho	*Jimmy John's**	**Oregon**	*Salt & Straw*
Illinois	*Lou Malnati's Pizzeria*	**Pennsylvania**	*Jim's Steaks*
Indiana	*Chatam Tap*	**Rhode Island**	*Gray's Ice Cream*
Iowa	*Dale Valley Winery*	**South Carolina**	*Zaxby's Chicken Fingers*
Kansas	*Call Hall Dairy Bar*	**South Dakota**	*Hitchrail Post*
Kentucky	*Original KFC*	**Tennessee**	*The Frothy Monkey*
Louisiana	*Original Raising Canes*	**Texas**	*Gourdough's*
Maine	*Duck Fat*	**Utah**	*Moochie's Meatballs*
Maryland	*B&O Brasserie*	**Vermont**	*Bragg Farm*
Massachusetts	*Toscanini's*	**Virginia**	*Sugar Shack Donuts*
Michigan	*Lafayette Coney Island*	**Washington**	*Din Tai Fung*
Minnesota	*Sebastian Joe's Ice Cream*	**West Virginia**	*The Empty Glass*
Mississippi	*Fenian's Pub*	**Wisconsin**	*Smoke Shack*
Missouri	*Crown Candy Kitchen*	**Wyoming**	*Winger's Roadhouse*

*I'm sure there are better spots in Idaho, but sadly this was the only place I ate at in the state.

24. WYOMING

Nature's Spa in Yellowstone
Yellowstone National Park. June 23, 2015

My left leg felt as if it was on fire and my right leg as if it was being frozen in a block of ice. I wasn't straddling the worlds created by George RR Martin,[52] but rather I was standing at the intersection of two rivers in Yellowstone National Park.

The river swarming my left side was the Boiling River, a small thermal water flow that sprang from the ground in Yellowstone. The river freezing my right side was the Gardner River, a tributary of the Yellowstone River coming from the peak of a nearby mountain.

In between the two, where the flowing temperatures crashed, was perfection. I ventured a little further before dropping my entire body into the natural spa and enjoyed the fluid jets of Earth's Jacuzzi.

This was one of only two places in Yellowstone you could legally swim and was quickly becoming my favorite spot in the park. David and I had spent the day driving throughout what will hopefully one day be called Mother Nature's Golden Palace, making pit stops at all the highlights: Old Faithful, the Grand Canyon of Yellowstone, and the Upper and Lower Falls.

And up until this point, I had been unimpressed with the world's first National Park.

---

52 The author of "A Song of Ice and Fire," not the doppelganger we saw in Iowa.

Ooooh, a small stream of water that jets up from the ground every hour and a half? So what? I can do the same thing in a pool by squeezing my hands together. *Aaah, a small canyon named after a bigger canyon I've already seen?* Show me more. *Ohhh, waterfalls that are far away and you can't even hike?* Let's stand around and look.

Admittedly, I was in a bit of a mood. Sure, there was wonderful nature all around us, but there were also a lot of people. And traffic. And stupid buffalo who kept turning their heads as I tried to take a selfie.

After ten days and more than 3,600 miles on our current road trip, "I've seen so many cool things" fatigue started to set in, and I was becoming numb to the novelty of nature. We had visited Kasha Katuwe, Bandelier, Garden of the Gods, Pikes Peak, Craters of the Moon, and now Yellowstone all within the last 120 hours. That was less time than that one guy had his arm stuck in a rock in the biopic, *Man Gets Arm Stuck in Rock.*[53]

Don't get me wrong; each location had its highlights, and each was worthy of a visit, but the impressiveness had started to wear off, and I was becoming desensitized to the beauty around me, a form of hedonic adaptation setting in.

It was a pro and a con of human resiliency. We quickly return to a relatively stable level of happiness in response to both positive and negative stimuli. This is good when something negative happens, as it doesn't affect you long term; it's not as good when something positive happens, and your response is "meh." It's why winning the lottery doesn't improve your long-term happiness and how we all manage to move on in our lives after the Buckeyes lose.

I had noticed both extremes on my trip so far. After my two-state self-pity tour in Mississippi and Arkansas, I found my stride as a nomad, and I accepted constant travel as my norm. I returned to my generally positive demeanor and enthusiastically embraced my decision.

Then I hit positive after positive, high on life moments one after another, and soon I was finding things to complain about that were clearly meme-worthy First World problems. Sure I was getting to see *World Atlas*'s #9 best national park in the world, but I had to wait for twenty minutes in traffic to do it!

But the convergence of the two different water sources washed me from my blasé mood. Perhaps it was because just minutes ago I was simultaneously freezing and on fire or, maybe, it was because, right now, the rivers felt like a liquid embrace of comfort. It was like when you finally found the right setting in the hotel shower. Too hot and you burn yourself; too cold and you freeze. But mix them together in just the right Goldilocks quantities, and you get the

---

53 Technically the movie was called *127 Hours*, but I think my title is better.

makings of a thirty-five-minute waterfall cleanse.

I leaned backward against the currents of the water; a firm footing on a rock kept me from being swept further downstream. If I shifted slightly to my left, the water got warmer; if I moved to my right, the water got cooler. I pendulummed back and forth between the two, enjoying the subtle changes in temperature and thought about nothing but the rivers on my skin.

I dropped my ears below the surface of the water, drowning out the sound of kids playing upstream and adults conversing to my left. I stared up at the empty blue sky and, as I lay in the water, found nirvana. Any stress or worries I had flowed downstream with the water; any desires or wants went right along with them. By focusing on that singular moment, nothing before and nothing after, I was able to step off the hedonic treadmill and just enjoy the present.

In a short while, I would head back to the car with David. We'd continue our journey on to Billings, Montana, en route to Mt. Rushmore the next day. We would get caught in a storm and have to do some backtracking and get stuck in a bit of traffic. We'd see more people, encounter more annoyances, and continue to fail to get a good buffalo selfie.

But none of that mattered right now; I was too busy doing nothing but enjoying the experience. I shifted back toward my left. *Oh yeah, that's the spot.*

25. SOUTH DAKOTA

Long Exposure
Badlands National Park. June 24, 2015

I stared up into the night sky, the only light coming from the stars and the moon above. All around us was the kind of dark you imagine exists but never see when you live in a big city, the kind where there's little difference between what you see whether your eyes are opened or closed.

David and I were lying on the roof of our rental car in the Badlands National Park in South Dakota. We had arrived shortly before dusk and had found a parking spot along the main road to take in the sunset and ensuing stargazing. We killed time playing with David's camera, taking long-exposure pictures in an attempt to capture some of the beauty we saw, but the images could do it no justice.

But now we were just looking up, silently, staring off into literal space. As the Earth rotated imperceptibly beneath us, I reflected on our time in South Dakota.

David and I started the day by visiting Mount Rushmore, a "see it so you can say you've seen it" stop on any great American road trip. In some ways, the rock carving of the four presidents was quite impressive, I mean, they took a giant rock and turned it into faces. And yet it was also much smaller than I expected. Had it not been for deciding to eat lunch at the cafeteria on site, we would have spent less than twenty minutes at the monument.

After that, we went to a show so that I could check off South Dakota. The only event we could find that day was a music open mic at a place called

Hitchrail Post in Pringle, South Dakota, population 112 (not 112,000, but 112 total).

When we pulled up to the bar, we had flashbacks to Iowa, as our perception was not reality. On the outside, the venue appeared to be a biker bar, a man in leather proudly displayed his gun as he rocked back and forth on the porch in front of a line of Harleys and a single regular bicycle.

On the inside was a beautiful space filled with wonderful people. Every person we met was equal parts incredibly friendly and side quest character from a role-playing game.

Our first interaction came from the bartender, a gray-haired lady in her mid-forties or fifties who welcomed us with a smile and a bit of friendly sass.

"What can I do you for?" she asked.

"Is there an open mic here today?" I inquired.

"That there is, buttercup. The host should be in around 4:30 p.m. Would you like anything to drink in the meantime?"

I ordered water, and David ordered a beer he didn't want, so we weren't shunned by the establishment. A bit later, a stout blond man entered the bar, and our bartender informed us that he was our host.

We followed the man into another room where he dropped off his guitar case, and we introduced ourselves. The man had an intimidatingly firm handshake but a friendly smile and introduced himself as Jeff. We later learned he was a former narcotics officer from Florida and a talented guitarist.

I signed up for the mic, we ordered some food, and we waited. While the minutes ticked by, we met a cowboy whose name I never learned. I knew he was a cowboy because he wore a cowboy hat, cowboy shoes, and sported an epic blonde handlebar mustache that extended an inch past his chin.

"What brings you to Pringle?" the cowboy asked.

"We're visiting all the states and just came in from Mount Rushmore. What about you?" I replied.

"Well, the cows brought me here, but it's the people who made me stay," the cowboy responded. I imagined a long piece of straw coming from his mouth as he talked.

"We read there's only 112 people in Pringle; do you like it?" I asked.

"Despite what they say in Texas, bigger ain't always better," he replied. "There might only be a hundred of us, but I'll be damned if they aren't some of the nicest hundred people you ever met."

I thought back to the biker sitting on the porch with a gun in his hand. Who's to say he wasn't one of the nicest people I'd ever meet?

Shortly after, Jeff kicked off the mic and introduced me to the stage. I repeated my performance from the poetry show in Florida, this time with an improved Dramatic Reading of Dumb Jokes and a more polished version of the Clichéd Meaning of Life. After my set, the audience of nice people shared their applause.

As I stepped off stage, a woman came directly at me. She had short black hair, two neck tattoos, and a few missing teeth. I had no idea what to expect.

"You were real good," she said. "I didn't get to see the first part of that, but that end thing you did was, man, it was just so good. I don't know who you are, but I am your newest fan."

I smiled and thanked her for her comments. We chatted a while longer before David and I left the Western saloon to continue our journey. We were headed toward Pierre when we decided to stop in the Badlands to see as much as we could before night fell. We arrived just in time to see the sun setting on the buttes and spires of the national park and then waited around for the stars.

And that's when I reflected.

It's something I enjoyed doing, a way of checking in on what I'm spending my time on and what I'm doing with my life. It's also probably why some of my favorite songs are about reflection: Michael Jackson's "Man in the Mirror," Justin Timberlake's "Mirror," and Mulan's "My Reflection."

The metaphor of taking a good look at ourselves is a powerful one. It's about being deliberate about who we are and what we do. That's why sometimes, when I wake up in the morning, I'll stand in front of my mirror and just reflect.[54]

As I continued my gaze to the stars above, I made out the Big Dipper, one of the few constellations I could spot without the help of an augmented reality app. I thought of Carl Sagan's *Pale Blue Dot*. Scientifically, we were all just a collection of cells on a rock hurtling through space, and humanity was but a blip on the timeline of existence. I was reminded of those internet videos that showed just how massive our universe was and how tiny we were in comparison, kind of like Pringle, South Dakota.

The 112 people of Pringle represented just 0.0000016 percent of the total human population on Earth; my newest fan with the two neck tattoos was but one of roughly 7,214,958,996 others on the planet. Most of those 7.2 billion had no idea that a place called Pringle existed. Heck, a majority of them didn't even know South Dakota existed. I realized that Earth was the Pringle of the universe, an infinitesimally small piece of a much larger puzzle.

The realization was equally comforting and not. In the grand scheme of things, it didn't matter that I had messed up a joke in my performance earlier that day. At the same time, it also may not matter at all what I do, ever.

What was the long-term value of my efforts to make people laugh or

---

54 You're welcome, again.

help them to do their jobs better while enjoying them more? What benefit did writing these words provide, not to me, but to existence as a whole? Were my puns as life-changing as I liked to believe?

The thought could seem depressing, but that was far too defeatist for me. If what we do each day doesn't mean much in the grand scheme of existence, then we might as well make it mean something for right now. The universe didn't care that I flubbed a line in a joke that day. It didn't care that I told any jokes at all. But the people of Pringle cared. They cared that I had made them laugh and made them think. They told me so. And that human-to-human impact was pretty awesome.

I felt good about my reflections, like when you have a really good hair day and give yourself a good wink when you notice it in the mirror. I took a deep breath as my eyes took in the night sky above. I waited for a shooting star to show that the cosmos agreed with my interpretation of our existence. It never came.

US Population in Pringle, South Dakota

The population of Pringle, South Dakota is only 112 people. Let's say they had a soccer team (with one coach) that decided they were moving to another state so that there were now just 100 people in Pringle. If those 100 people reflected the population of the United States:

- 12 of those people would be from California, 9 would be from Texas, 6 would be Floridian, and 6 would be New Yorkers. One person would be a quarter South Dakotan, and one person's arm would be a Wyominger.
- 81 people would live in the "town" of Pringle while 19 would live in rural areas.
- 64 people would be white, 16 would be Hispanic, 12 would be black, and 8 people would be either Asian, Native American, or some other race. There would be no way of telling if anyone was actually a cylon.
- 71 people would identify as Christian, 4 would be agnostic, 3 would be atheist, 2 would be Jewish, 1 would be Muslim, 1 would be Hindu, 1 would be Buddhist, and 16 would say "nothing."
- 29 people would be Democrat, 26 would be Republican, and 42 would be Independent.
- 63 people would be adults (age 18 to 64), 23 would be eighteen or under, and 14 would be super old (65 or older). JK senior citizens!
- 51 people would be women; 49 would be men.
- 16 people would be immigrants, 8 would be children of immigrants, and 76 would be at least third-generation US citizens.
- 26 people would be obese, 21 would smoke, and 11 would have diabetes. The number of people who vaped would not stop talking about vaping.
- 10 people would control 77 percent of the wealth. 1 person would control 42 percent of it.
- 56 people would have pets, 31 would have cats, and 37 would have dogs because more people know that dogs are better than cats.
- 92 people would have a cellphone; 68 would have a smartphone. Which means 24 people would be walking around with old-school flip phones.
- One hair follicle on one of these people would be me, writing about the one hundred people in the town.

Sources:
"The United States as 100 People" by Alex Kuzoian. *Business Insider*, May 12, 2016
"Demography of the United States." Wikipedia, accessed December 1, 2016

26. NORTH DAKOTA

The Best Thing in North Dakota
Fargo, ND. June 26, 2015

I opened the doors, and I could've sworn I heard angels sing. This was what people must see when they have near-death experiences. I wasn't in heaven, but I was close. I was at Sandy's Donuts in Fargo, North Dakota.

Just twelve hours earlier, I was convinced that North Dakota was the boringest place on the planet, the geographic equivalent of watching paint dry while standing in a never-moving line with no internet-enabled phone. Basically, the worst.

That's no knock against North Dakotans; it's just a fact. North Dakota is home to two of the top-ten longest straight roads in the world. There are stretches of nothingness so vast your only hope is the sweet release of death, which you won't get in the summer because there's nothing to die from.

David and I started our Dakotan nonadventure the day before by driving from Pierre, South Dakota to Bismarck, North Dakota. In that stretch of two hundred miles, the only thing noteworthy was crossing the North/South border and seeing the state signs. South Dakota clung strongly to Mount Rushmore with the motto "Great Faces, Great Places." North Dakota promoted just one word: "Legendary."

After stopping briefly at the bland state capitol building in Bismarck, we made our way east on I-94 toward Fargo. And that's where things started to get exciting. First, at exit 257, was something absolutely bonkers: a left exit! That's right, after a mere hundred miles of nothing, we had the excitement of exiting on the left side of the highway if we wanted. We didn't because there was nothing worth exiting for, but having the option was thrilling.

Just one exit later, was Jamestown, home of the world's largest buffalo statue, a sixty-ton, anatomically correct figure named Dakota Thunder. We stopped to be mildly ambivalent about the giant buffalo and found that it sat in the middle of a fake town that commemorated days of yore, complete with a fake saloon, fake sheriff's office, fake dentist, and fake enthusiasm.

We made our way further east to Fargo, where we had a decent meal, saw a movie, and checked into a standard hotel. Little did we know the true wonders the thirty-ninth state of the union would bring us in the morrow.

Some philosophers suggest that happiness equals reality minus expectations. The thinking is that when reality surpasses our expectations, we are happy. When reality fails to meet our expectations, we're disappointed.

It's like *The Matrix* movies. No one had any expectations for the first movie when it premiered, it was incredible, so we were all really happy with it. By the time *Revolutions* came out, expectations were sky-high, it was meh, and I'm still upset I wasted those 129 minutes in the theater.

So, should everyone be pessimistic and assume the worst? Should we all be like Calvin who said, "I find my life is a lot easier the lower I keep everyone's expectations?"[55]

Not necessarily. According to a study published in *The Atlantic*—the newspaper, not a message in a bottle dropped in the ocean—negative emotions have an immediate payoff by protecting us, but positive emotions yield better results over time.

All of this to say that expectations play a role in our level of contentment, which is why North Dakota was about to make me ludicrously happy.

The next day started like most other days on our "Middle of the Country" road trip: David awoke first and showered while I clung to dreamland for an extra twenty minutes of sleep. Once he finished, he woke me up, and I showered. We packed our things, grabbed a pastry from the continental breakfast, and headed to our first event or activity of the day.

That morning, it was a speaking engagement for students at North Dakota State University. The talk went well, and the students were positive in their feedback, both written and nonverbal. They had been engaged, excited, and eager to laugh at my jokes, which means they were the best kind of audience. After the event, Kelli, our contact at the university, uttered possibly the most important sentence that has ever been spoken in the state: "Before you

---

55 This is Calvin from *Calvin and Hobbes,* not John Calvin, the sixteenth-century French Reformation theologian.

leave, you have to try Sandy's Donuts."[56]

And it was there, at Sandy's Donuts in Fargo, North Dakota that I heard angels sing.

I walked toward the counter before having to stop in awe of its beauty. Rows upon rows of donuts were lit up with a yellow aura; halos of confectionary deliciousness, and heavenly decadence lined the wire shelves.

As I approached, I began to fully appreciate the breadth and depth of this particular donut experience. The names of the donuts were simple, a sign that Sandy knew he didn't need fancy marketing language to sell his goods; the taste did that for him. The selection was as wide as it was delicious: glazed, chocolate, sugar twist, apple cluster, M&M, PB frosted cinnamon roll, and so much more. But the donut of all donuts sat in the bottom case, left side, middle row. There, in all its glory, was the S'mores Long John.

David and I ordered a couple of donuts each and took our seat. As we did, a cop car pulled up outside and two police officers walked in, the unofficial stamp of approval for any donut shop. They were clearly there to arrest their hunger.

I took the S'mores Long John in my hand, my mouth watering with anticipation. I bit in and my taste buds danced with the scrumptiousness of the ambrosia in my mouth. Fried dough mixed with marshmallow icing smothered my tongue while chocolate and graham cracker circled back for a second hit of sugary ecstasy. I spent the next few moments silent, unable to fully process this heaven on a platter before me.

As I finished the long john, I felt awash with euphoria. Despite my first (and second [and probably third]) impression, I loved North Dakota. It wasn't because I spoke at a university and checked off a state, and it wasn't because I got to see a giant statue in a fake town. It was because of this donut.

And the state had set it up perfectly. Tales of the boringness of North Dakota rang true at first, the utter nothingness on the highway keeping expectations low. Slowly, reality improved with each experience, until *boom* an incredible donut right in the kisser, a happy ending to a not-so-fairy tale.

I finally understood the state's slogan; it was clearly talking about Sandy's Donuts. Legendary.

---

56 A close second is probably something Theodore Roosevelt said while ranching there, considering he claimed the state was critical for him becoming president.

27. MINNESOTA

Life Is a Roller Coaster
Minneapolis, MN. June 26, 2015

We waited patiently in the queue. Fortunately, there were only two people ahead of us, so the wait wouldn't be long. David and I were in our last state before we'd make our way back to Ohio, and our "Middle of the Country" road trip would be over. We had covered more than 5,000 miles, fifteen states, and twelve stories.

Our last state would be a doozy, complete with meeting up with good friends, eating some delicious food, and performing in an awesome show at CSz Twin Cities. But the real highlight was what we were in line for: a roller coaster in the Mall of America in Minneapolis, Minnesota.

The Mall is huge. It's the largest mall in the United States at 4.87 million square feet. It hosts 40 million visitors annually and contains 500-plus stores, a comedy club, a bowling alley, an arcade, a chapel (where more than 7,000 people have gotten married), an aquarium, and twenty-seven rides, including five legit roller coasters. All indoors kept at a comfortable seventy degrees.[57]

We had visited the mall for a quick lunch and decided we couldn't pass up the opportunity to roller coast while inside, so we grabbed some tickets and thought about which ride we wanted to experience. Do we go with Avatar Air Bender or Shredder's Mutant Masher? Or maybe our thrills lay with the

---

57 That's seventy degrees Fahrenheit. I realize seventy degrees Celsius would not be comfortable at all.

Pepsi Orange Streak since we all equate thrills with soda.

Ultimately, we settled on Fairly Odd Coaster based on its description: "A hilarious misadventure providing hairpin turns, plummeting spirals, and speeding tracks." It wasn't the most extreme coaster in the middle of the mall, but it seemed to be the right balance between "this will be fun" and "this won't make me vomit the Great Steak I just ate."

The people in front of us were excitedly waiting their turn. They were two young girls, somewhere between the ages of six and sixteen (I'm terrible at estimating ages). The people behind us were equally excited. They were three young professionals sporting the unmistakable look of business attire, clearly on their lunch break from a nearby office job. Their ties said they were professionals; their excitement said they were human.

As we waited, I was reminded of our summers at Kings Island, an awesome amusement park just north of Cincinnati, Ohio. Early on, our trips to KI were a whole family outing. I'd ask my mom to let me wear my "tall shoes" so I had better luck getting onto the rides and would walk on my tippy toes when they measured my height to seal the deal.

By the time I was a teenager, we had season passes and would spend seemingly our entire summer at the amusement park, riding The Beast, Vortex, King Cobra, and countless others. I should clarify: I would ride all those rides—David, not so much. He was terrified of heights and refused to ride anything he thought involved going higher than a two-story building.

One summer, I convinced him that one of the rides, The Adventure Express, didn't have a steep drop. The first time riding it, he freaked out as we climbed the first hill only for that fear to turn into fun upon eclipsing the hill and seeing that it was a more gradual decline. We spent that entire summer riding that one ride over and over again. Eventually, The Adventure Express became David's gateway coaster, and he's on board with riding them now as an adult.

As we waited for our metal adventure to begin, I thought about how my nomadic experience was much like the experience of riding a roller coaster. It was a cliché metaphor to be sure, but I didn't mean it how most people do. The way most people use that analogy isn't even a good one.

First, most people ignored what make roller coasters fun. Sure, they have ups and downs, but the downs are the fun part. No one rides a coaster thinking, "Oh man, I can't wait until the car is slowly going up." No, you ride the coaster for when you've reached your peak, something that may take a little while to do, and then everything goes downhill, fast.

That's a terrible metaphor for life: "Be sure to work really hard so that you have a lot of fun when it all quickly spirals out of control."

Second, people only reference the ride itself: "Life is a roller coaster; it has its ups and downs." Well yeah, but that's only part of the experience. Most of the time spent rollercoastering is spent waiting in line. And this was perhaps the more apt metaphor for my journey.

So often, we only focus on the ups and downs, the things that are thrilling because they're fun or because they're terrifying. Life has a lot of in-between time, where things just are. But no one talks about that. Nobody Instagrams waiting in line; they take a picture once they're on the ride.

When people asked me about my time as a nomad, they wanted to know about the ups and the downs. "What was the best state you went to? What was the worst? Did you have any good food? What was the coolest thing you saw? What was the hardest part?"

No one wanted to hear about the boring moments in between those stories, but they existed, and they accounted for more of my time than the exciting ones. As my editor would ask me countless times in my first draft: "Why are you telling this story?" My answer couldn't be, "because it happened" or "because I need to put something down for West Virginia." North Dakota was only a story because it ended in deliciousness. Who would want to read an entire write-up of a boring drive that ended just as a boring drive? Heck, who would want to write it?[58]

But life isn't a book or a movie. It's not just about the ups and the downs of the ride; it's about the time spent leading up to those moments. And if you only focus on the extremes, you miss a lot in the middle.

The closest comparison I could think of was the clichéd reality that life is about the journey *and* the destination. The people who were happiest were those who found ways to enjoy that time in the middle, that time when things weren't incredible and they weren't awful. They learned to enjoy the wait as well as the ride.

My thoughts on life were interrupted by the click of a harness. I hadn't even noticed that the line had moved and we had sat down into our Fairly Odd seats.

As the coaster started forward, I took out my phone—something I would later get yelled at for by ride operator—so I could record the ride. People on Instagram would want to see this![59]

---

58 Except for maybe J.R.R. Tolkien. He could've described anything for a hundred pages, and we'd all wait to see Peter Jackson turn it into a movie.

59 To see the now ironic video of me riding Fairly Odd Coaster, visit tarv.in/minnesota

28. MICHIGAN

Michigan Is the Worst
Detroit, MI. August 1, 2015

I hate people from Michigan. I have to; I'm from Ohio and went to *The Ohio State University*. But I don't hate them because of the rivalry between the schools or the fact that the states once went to war over the city of Toledo.[60]

The real reason I hate Michiganders is that they are in love with the fact that their state is shaped like a hand. You ask anyone where they're from in Michigan, and they'll hold up their hand, "Well if this is Michigan, I'm from right here." People from other places don't do that. When people ask me where I'm from, I don't make a makeshift Ohio by curling my knuckles and say, "Well if this is Ohio, I'm from the *abductor pollicis brevis*." People from Italy aren't like, "Well if Italy is a boota, I'ma from the stiletto."[61]

And so I sat, with disdain, at the top of a slide in Belle Isle in Detroit, Michigan, waiting for something tragic to happen so I could justify my hatred of the Mitten State.

I was at the city park on a disgustingly beautiful summer Saturday, the

---

60 It's true, the state of Ohio went to war with the territory of Michigan over the Toledo strip in 1835. The "war" culminated in a single military confrontation with a report of shots being fired in the air but no casualties. Michigan ended up ceding Toledo in exchange for additional land and statehood, but it set the stage for the Greatest Rivalry in Sports: Michigan versus Ohio State in college football.

61 I'm sorry if this representation of Italian is offensive to anyone; I only know a little Italian. His name is Tony.

weather a stupid 80 degrees. The sun was shining, and a light breeze made the whole ordeal even more sickening in its joyful perfection. To my right was Jaclynn, a member of CSz Detroit and my Michigan tour guide for the day. Unfortunately, she's also one of the nicest people on the planet.

It was my first new state in nearly a month. After my brotherly road trip, I spent most of July in Ohio, New York, Pennsylvania, and DC for speaking engagements, stand-up shows, and more calzones at LaRosa's. But now I was back to my states tour, starting with what I was sure would be the worst state in the union. Much to my dismay, I had already had a good time in Michigan, and the slide would surely only make things worse.

The day before I was in Ann Arbor, where I walked around the University of Michigan, upset that the campus was beautiful and not dilapidated, as I had hoped. That night, I did a stand-up set on a show that a good comedy friend of mine from New York, Nore Davis, happened to be headlining. The jerks had the nerve to laugh at my jokes.

Then there was the monstrosity that was that Saturday. Jaclynn and I started the day by visiting Lafayette Coney Island, one of the two famous Coney hot dog places in the city. Sadly, the food was edible, though it wasn't as good as Skyline in Cincinnati. At least one thing was working out.

And then we were off to Belle Isle, where things had gone from bad to worse by going from good to great. We walked past an open field with the horrendous sound of kids playing and people having fun. We frustratingly rekindled the days of our youth as we took a turn on the monkey bars. And we had found this dumb, fun slide.

I wish I could say it was a small, measly slide infected with tetanus. But no, it was one of those giant ones where you hike three flights of stairs to get to the top, put your feet into a burlap sack, and push off.

While I sat at the top of what was sure to be a fun experience on a beautiful summer day, I knew that if I was going to hate my time in Detroit, it would have to be because of a bad experience, not because the city was inherently awful like I had assumed. I was hopeful that I might get concussed as we raced down the metal lanes of the slide, or that I'd accidentally wipe out a kid on the way down and get locked up for involuntary child kicking, or that I'd at least get a weird rash or something. None of those things would happen.

I'm sure somewhere in this whole debacle of a day was the realization that it was wrong to hate an entire location because of a sports rivalry and silly to judge an entire populace because they used their hand to show where they lived. But the narrative that Michigan sucked had long been ingrained in me as an Ohio native, OSU grad, and decent human being.

I knew that visiting new places had the ability to change your perspective, challenge your assumptions, and reduce your prejudice; it was one of the things I enjoyed most about traveling. If people traveled more, they might hate others less. I just didn't want that to be true about Michigan, and I certainly didn't want "learning a lesson" to be added to the things this dumb state had provided. Sadly, the lesson was forcing itself into my brain.

A little later we would be going to get pizza from a local spot named Buddy's—which luckily wasn't on par with LaRosa's—before I would begrudgingly play in a fun ComedySportz show. We would follow that disappointment with a night of karaoke with the whole cast where I would, unfortunately, be doomed to having a good time.

But at that moment, a three-story slide awaited. As the attendant gave the go-ahead sign, I scooted forward to let gravity do its thing. I tried desperately to hide the smile this awful joy was providing me. I slid down the metal slope with ease and delight. As I neared the bottom, I hoped for a broken bone or at least a splinter so I could have been justified in hating this place, but I'll be darned if I didn't land gracefully.

This truly was the worst thing Michigan could have done: I wanted to hate it, but it wouldn't let me. Michigan was the worst.

29. GEORGIA

How to Google How to Use Bath Salts
Savannah, GA. August 7, 2015

I didn't think about the implications as I typed the question into Google. If I had, I certainly would have used incognito mode or would have at least been more specific in my query. The results on the screen quickly revealed my naiveté. It seems very few people who google "how to use bath salts" were in the same predicament as me.

I was in Mansion Forsythe, a fancy hotel, in Savannah, Georgia. Earlier that day I had delivered a keynote to a nonprofit group on the value of humor at work, and this was the hotel they had booked for me.

The building itself was as grandiose as it was gorgeous. It was a Victorian Romanesque mansion converted into a hotel, catering to senior executives, rich couples, and me. It sat across from Forsythe Park and was walking distance from Savannah's River Street, described on their website as a "glittering, multi-faceted gem along the broad Savannah River" that is home to "century-old buildings that have been converted to antique shops, distinctive boutiques, spectacular galleries, quaint brew pubs, and fabulous restaurants." This is presumably better than having distinctive shops, spectacular boutiques, quaint galleries, fabulous brew pubs, and antique restaurants.

My room in the Vict-Ro mansion was immaculate. Not only did it seem larger than any of my NYC apartments, it also had better decor than anything I had kept or thrown away the day I became a nomad. I imagined if my house had looked like this, it probably would have been harder to leave it all behind.

The furniture was all distinctly not from Ikea, built by actual furnitur-ists with woodworking skills and more tools than just an Allen wrench. The king-size bed was adorned with pillows filled with clouds and was covered in a comforter as warm as a loved one's embrace. A classy red lounge chair sat next to the bed, just waiting for a distinguished gentleman to sit down with a ma-jestic briar pipe in hand (but not in mouth as the hotel had a strict no-smok-ing policy). On the marble-topped desk sat a candelabra, like the French actor from *Beauty and the Beast*.

But the highlight for me was that the bathroom was a literal bath room, as it had a bathtub in it. Having spent the last seven years living in NYC, the sight of a bathtub was a rare thing. And this was no ordinary tub for bathing. It was a "luxurious oversized claw-foot soaking tub."

Naturally, I decided to treat myself.

To make things even more soak-worthy, the front desk person had kindly given me a cup of bath salts to enhance the experience. How she knew I want-ed to sit naked in a giant bowl of water was beyond me; maybe I just had that kind of face.

The problem was, I didn't know how to use the bath salts. I've used bub-ble bath before, and I knew what to do with a rubber ducky in the tub, but pulverized minerals were new to me.

Do you pour them in while the water is running? Or after? Or before you even start? Maybe you rub them on your body as you soak. What do they even do? Do they exfoliate the skin or prevent that weird wrinkling of your fingers when you're in the water for too long? Do you have to throw some over your shoulder to ward off bad luck? What were they for?

With so many questions, I turned to the smartest person I know: Goo-gle. It's one of the benefits of living in the Information Age: anything you could possibly want to learn is just a search away.

Want to know how far you are from the closest Shake Shack? Google it. Experiencing *presque vu* and can't think of an actor's name? Google it. Don't know what *presque vu* means? Google. It.[62]

But as I looked at the results of "how to use bath salts," it seemed fewer people were concerned with having a soothing, relaxing bath, and more were interested in finding a quick hit that leads to a brief feeling of euphoria that turns into anxiety, agitation, aggression, hallucinations, suicidal thoughts,

---

62 Or you can look right here: *presque vu* is one of the three *vus* used to describe different phenomenon. Most people know *déjà vu*, when you feel like you've experienced something before. *Jamais vu* is the opposite where you experience a situation you recognize in some way but it is still unfamiliar. *Presque vu* is when you know you know something you just can't seem to retrieve it in that exact moment, aka "tip of the tongue." *Déjà vu* is when you feel like you've experienced something before.

kidney failure, and possible spontaneous breakdown of muscle fiber.

To be clear: the latter set of symptoms come from ingesting a drug called bath salts, not from sitting in a tub with fancified water.

I made a few tweaks to my Google search and found the instructions I needed, spontaneous breakdown of muscle fiber not included.

I turned the water on in the tub and waited until it was about halfway to the desired level. I sprinkled the cup of bath salts over the length of the tub and watched them float to the bottom of the porcelain. When the water finished filling, I lowered myself into bathing position.

I closed my eyes and let the stress of the past few days of travel soak away. I had gone from Michigan to Ohio to Missouri to Illinois to New York to Georgia in six days and was heading to Texas in the morning to complete a nice "seven in seven" travel week. But for now, I soaked.

As the bath salts exfoliated my epidermis and, according to one woman's Facebook post, "eliminated pollutants and toxins from my skin," I had a worrying thought: What if travel was my bath salts; what if it was my drug? What if I was traveling for that quick hit of euphoria and then moving on to the next spot before I had a chance to crash?

Drugs are often used as an escape, and my nomadic trip had become an escape from my real life. I didn't have to invest as heavily in relationships because I had the excuse that I was on the road. I didn't have to have the hard conversations because I was leaving the next morning. I didn't have to be responsible for anyone but myself.

And people were cheering me on to do it, like a group of friends laughing about how crazy Joe gets when he's blackout-drunk, despite the fact he's clearly become an alcoholic.

I used to do stand-up about how I was waiting to do drugs for when I was much older. As a youngin, I can still travel, go on adventures, and see the world. I was saving acid trips for when they were the only kind of trip I could take. But maybe I was already taking drugs by taking off.

I sank further into the tub, recreating the experience of lying in the rivers of Yellowstone. Travel couldn't be my drug because I wasn't addicted, right?

Things I've Googled

Given how frequently we use Google to answer any question that comes to mind, a person's search history is one of the most private things they have, right up there with their social security number, fingerprints, and how they use the bathroom. During the eighteen months I lived as a nomad, I made 10,198 searches on Google. For a peek inside my mind, here are some of the things I was searching for:

- March 1, 2015 at 01:17—how to undo a stripped screw
- April 7, 2015 at 19:24—leonardo dicaprio boys club
- May 19, 2015 at 23:09—how to sleep in a car
- June 8, 2015 at 21:45—want to hear a dirty joke a boy fell in the mud
- July 13, 2015 at 20:46—pale in comparison
- August 7, 2015 at 21:13—how to use bath salts
- September 7, 2015 at 10:50—music make you lose control
- October 22, 2015 at 12:40—impact of improv on creativity
- November 4, 2015 at 20:43—pronounce homonymous hemianopsia
- December 24, 2015 at 16:34—christmas weave
- January 1, 2016 at 02:26—new year's grapes tradition
- February 10, 2016 at 11:23—recommended spf for hawaii
- March 16, 2016 at 15:39—how to adjust to time change when in asia
- April 4, 2016 at 02:00—btfo
- May 12, 2016 at 19:16—what are the fence things in wyoming
- June 6, 2016 at 16:13—how to become a lord
- July 4, 2016 at 22:22—there's a monster at the end of this book
- August 31, 2016 at 19:37—how to estimate radiation from miles flown

30. TEXAS

A Series of Minor Inconveniences
Houston, TX. August 9, 2015

The giggles started around midnight.

I was in my bed in my hotel room in Houston, Texas, and the man in the room next to me was laughing. Not laughing like the adult man he was, but rather like a 'roided out toddler playing extreme peek-a-boo.

Under normal circumstances, this probably would have been funny. In fact, most days, any of the things that had happened to me in the last twelve hours would have been funny, or even more likely, not even noticed. But not that day. That day, the laughter was just another item in a long list of the stupidity that was my nomadic existence, and I was so annoygry that I was willing to make up a portmanteau that was much worse than hangry.

The first annoyance started that morning when my plane landed at IAH. As soon as the "you can finally stand up now" bing of the airplane sounded, everyone stood up. One passenger from the back starting pushing her way forward instead of waiting and exiting by rows, ignoring the unwritten rules of disembarking a plane that were likely established by the Wright brothers themselves. I thought little of it at the time except, "That lady sucks."

The second annoyance came from that same woman seconds later as she made it to the jet bridge. One of her bags shifted off her shoulder, and she decided to stop in the middle of the exit tube to adjust her carrying technique, leaving no room for anyone to make their way around. The whole process took no more than fifteen seconds, but that was long enough for me to let out a sigh. Here we go.

The next frustration occurred as I made the long trek to the airport exit, and people committed one of the greatest crimes against humanity: they stood on the left side of the escalator. I'm not a violent person, but nothing makes me want to punch someone in the kidney as much as them forcing their laziness on me by standing on the left on an escalator. Please, just stand out of the way, so those of us with things to do can get on our frustrated way.

Irritation *numero cuatro* happened as soon as I stepped outside of the airport when I was hit with the oppressive heat that is Houston in August: a balmy 99 degrees. One more degree and you had triple digits; one less and you had a boy band.

Strike number five occurred shortly after I got to the rental car pickup. After a lengthy wait, it was finally my turn at the counter. I initialed all the boxes on the contract to confirm I read the things I definitely didn't read, I declined insurance coverage 800 times, and was pointed toward my car, located across the parking lot in spot #72. I made my way back outside in the heat and down to #72, only to find no car there. I walked through the non-air-conditioned parking lot looking for the license plate of my rental and came up empty. That meant a trip back to the office, another wait, and a new car, this time in spot #92.

When I unlocked my car, I got to vexation number six: the musty smell of a car that had clearly been smoked in despite being a non-smoking vehicle. Of course, I unfairly thought, everyone in Texas smokes.

Frustration number seven took place on the roads: did everyone need to drive a pickup truck on heightened suspensions? What could you possibly be doing that justifies needing a ladder to get into your vehicle?

After getting through the Monster Truck Pep Rally that is Houston traffic (#8), I made it to my hotel in downtown Houston, where I was met with irritation number nine: having to swipe my card five times before it unlocked the door to my room. If aliens ever invaded Earth, I'm sure they would laugh at our continued use of fossil fuels and our inability to make a card-based lock that works the first time.

Moments later, perturbance *nummer zehn* reverberated in my ears as my hotel phone started ringing far too loudly. It was guest services welcoming me to the hotel and telling me to the let them know if I needed anything. It was a nice gesture but entirely unnecessary. Would I not know what to do if I needed something and they hadn't called? Didn't the front desk person welcome me already? How many germs did I just pick up by touching that phone? You could take your hospitality, Front Desk Lady, and shove it.

And so the day continued, minor annoyance stacking on top of minor annoyance, driving me to the brink of insanity. There was slow Wi-Fi, over-priced hotel food, boring conference calls, a crappy weight room, zero water pressure, more traffic, pointless emails, long lines, and on and on and on.

And then there were the giggles—the irritating sound of a man being happy—and I couldn't take it.

Houston, usually, is a great city, one I've been to many times before and have thoroughly enjoyed. I've eaten at delicious restaurants like Bombay Pizza Kitchen and visited awesome spots like Buffalo Bayou Park. In fact, I've had great experiences all across the state of Texas, from eating at tasty spots like Torchy's Tacos, Gourdough's, and the easternmost In N Out, to performing in ComedySportz shows in Houston, Dallas, and San Antonio. I've delivered events for great universities like Texas A&M, companies like Santander, and conferences like the Women's Foodservice Forum, all in the Lone Star State. And I've experienced the finer points of Texan culture at the State Fair of Texas, whatever the heck Midnight Yell is at A&M, and—how could I forget?—the Alamo.

Once you get over the overzealous pride of the state, their propensity for country music, and can avoid the racists that sadly still exist, Texas was a wonderful place. Just like the rest of the country.

That's what made traveling so much fun. Seeing what each state had to offer was exciting, meeting new people was enriching, and working with different organizations was fulfilling. Flying from place to place and sleeping in different hotel rooms across the country was great. Until it wasn't.

One of the keys to motivation, as Charles Duhigg says, is to turn a chore into a choice. Taking a moment to understand how a specific activity you have to do connects to the larger goals you want to do makes it easier for us to take action.

Going into work is easier when you remember that you're doing it to provide a comfortable living for your family. Scheduling a doctor's appointment becomes a higher priority when you're reminded it will help you live longer. Waking up early isn't hard when it's to see the sunrise, go for a hike, or when it's Christmas morning and you're eagerly waiting to receive a Nintendo.

But what happens when your choice becomes a chore? What happens when "I *get* to fly to Houston today" becomes "I *have* to fly to Houston today," when getting on a flight isn't to see the world but just a part of your commute?

You're frustrated you had to sit in traffic to get to work? I had to sit on a plane that was stuck on the runway for forty minutes because they couldn't get the bathroom light to work correctly. Oh, you hit some construction on your way home and had to take a detour on a route you know? I had to guess my way through a city I've never been to because Google Maps kept telling me to take the one route that was blocked off.

None of the Houston strikes were awful by themselves. They weren't even awful summed together. They were just annoying, and that's what made it worse. They were First World problems that I had no right to even complain about.

Friend and fellow speaker Jason Kotecki jokes that speakers are the only people who will hear about some tragedy that has befallen a peer and think, "Oh my god, you're so lucky. Your house caught on fire, you lost your arm, and you have a flesh-eating disease? You basically have your keynote written for you."

He's joking—we speakers don't want bad things to happen; we can also tell stories about good things. It's just that if things go wrong, we want them to go wrong enough that we can at least talk about them in an interesting way.

That's what made this trip so awful. It was nothing catastrophic, just a series of minor inconveniences. And these small things happened every single day on the road, and I was getting tired of it. As the giggles started fading away, I realized that if travel was my drug, I was crashing.

31. ARIZONA

Alone Atop the Rock
Grand Canyon North Rim. August 14, 2015

I walked across the narrowing rock peninsula toward my destination. On either side of me was canyon, dropping thousands of feet below. In front of me was a rock expanse that I knew would be the perfect spot to see an unobstructed view of the north side of the Grand Canyon. What I didn't know was how that view would make me feel.

I was at Point Imperial, the highest overlook at the North Rim and was taking a short break from a session of Speakers in Cars Getting Coaching, my made-up title for what my trip with Michelle, a fellow nomad and speaker, had become. We saw beautiful sights, ate great food, and helped each other with our businesses while exploring the wonders of Arizona.

Our coaching session that morning had gone well. As we made the drive to the North Rim, she helped me think through the structure of my full-day humor masterclass, and I helped her add some humor to her next speech. It was already a productive day, but by the time we reached Point Imperial, my introvertedness was kicking in, and I was in need of some time to recharge on my own. So Michelle and I took a break and went off separately to do our own things.

I made my way across the strait and started up the embankment. I climbed the dry dirt only to pause when I got to the top of the rock, struck by the view that was before me. The sky above was the quintessential blue that only a sky—and an aptly named crayon—can be. It was littered with clouds that I no longer knew the name for (Cumulus? Magna cum u lus?), with the afternoon sun hanging in the distance.

At eye level were the green pine trees of the North Rim, a layer of dark green reminiscent of mold in a bathtub that hadn't been cleaned in a long time, but in a weirdly beautiful way. Below was the majesty of the Grand Canyon, layers of color sprouting from the red rock, white stone, and specks of foliage dotting the ridges, painted by millions of years of erosion.

I was seeing one of the greatest views this Earth had to offer, and I was alone. Not "allllll by myseeeeeellyeeelf" lonely, but "there is no one around me" alone. It gave me a chance to think, to explore the thoughts bouncing around in my head, and to take a break from having to put together coherent sentences that had to make sense.

As I scanned the panorama, I felt like I was in *The Lion King*, like I was standing on Pride Rock where Simba was lifted out to the world. The clouds above reminded me of how *spoiler alert* after Mufasa died, he came to Simba in a vision in the sky.

I remembered my own father, who passed away a couple of years before, and the serenity of the moment brought with it a wave of emotion.

My dad never got to see this view. In his fifty-nine years, he never saw the beauty of the Grand Canyon or the redwoods of California or anything outside of North America for that matter. And there were countless people just like him, never having the opportunity, or perhaps inclination, to see the world beyond their hometown doorstep.

Guilt built in my body. A few days before I was complaining about my circumstances—woe was I for "having" to travel to so many beautiful locations. I felt unworthy of the life I had created.

Why did I deserve to see this view when so many others couldn't, or wouldn't, their entire life? What made me worthy of the opportunity to travel to all fifty states and beyond when others struggled just to get by, day to day, as my dad had struggled for the past few years before his death?

A stroke at the age of fifty-seven had left my father half-blind in each eye and unable to lift his hands above his shoulders. Overnight, his reality was ripped from him, and he could no longer do just about anything he loved. Working construction? Gone. Playing golf? Gone. Reading a book? Gone. And a little over a year after that stroke, he was gone.

I was the second person in my family to graduate college after my brother, David. My starting salary at P&G was more than what either of my parents earned when I graduated. At the age of thirty-one, I was living as a nomad, taking care of only myself. At thirty-one, my parents were raising three kids, paying a mortgage, and doing everything they could to give us what they never had.

They spent their entire adult lives working as hard as they could to support me and my brothers, and they had given up so much. But did I deserve it? Was I worthy of their sacrifice?

The guilt turned into sadness, a mourning for my father I hadn't felt since I first learned of his passing. I was on a train from NYC to Boston when my brother, Adam, called to give me the news. I had been worrying about the "stress" of delivering a good talk while my father was in a hospital bed in Cincinnati, fighting for his life. I sat ignorant to his struggles as he succumbed to pneumonia, a complication from the stroke, just two days after his fifty-ninth birthday.

Now, here I was, eighteen months after his death, with a view he would never see, an experience he would never have, and a story he would never hear. A smell of onions had apparently wafted through the canyon (and apparently my office as I typed this) because tears started streaming down my face.

My father, with all his flaws, had helped make me the person I was today. His sacrifice, encouragement, work ethic, and genes had given me the ability to go to college, get an education, start my own company, and explore the world. If he could only see me now.

I took in the view once again, one of the most beautiful I'd ever seen. The sadness turned to hope. Maybe, in a way, my dad was seeing the Grand Canyon now, through his son's eyes. Not in a weird, "I'm a ghost, boooooo" way, or even a spirit-in-heaven way. But my memory of him was there with me in that moment, as if he were by my side, waiting to make the perfect dad joke.

"Do you see this beautiful canyon, Dad?"

"I see, said the blind man, who picked up the hammer and saw. "

I smiled at the thought.

The breeze atop the rock picked up, and I thought about my mom, who I knew would love to experience a moment like this, to see something so beautiful, and I vowed to bring her here as soon I could.[63] Though I loved my father, we were never really close. My mom and I were. And it was the two of them who had given me everything I needed to get to where I was, standing on that rock.

I was sad, happy, disappointed, and proud all at the same time. I was

---

63 I did in fact encourage my mom to go to the Grand Canyon after the trip. I told her she should "definitely see it while she still could." She made fun of me for implying that she was old and may die soon. That wasn't my intent, I just meant while she was still spry. She gave me crap about it for nearly a year before we finally made it to the Grand Canyon. During one of the more challenging hikes, she said I was right to push to do it soon because she may not have survived it if we had waited much longer.

sad I wasn't sharing this view with the people I loved but happy I had seen it myself to tell them about it. I was disappointed my dad would never get to see this or get to hear about this trip or the countless others I went on as a nomad, but proud he had helped me become a man who could do those things and more.

I decided that if my parents had done so much for me to get to where I was, I owed it to them to make wherever that was worth it. The trip was no longer about just me; it was no longer just a checklist for me to complete, a travel high to experience, or something fun to do.

Travel wasn't a drug I was using to escape from the world or a chore I had resigned myself to do. Travel was a catalyst I was using to, as Mufasa might say, remember who I was. And if my dad could no longer see the world, I would see it for him.

I stood quietly for the next few minutes just taking in the experience, the wind whisking away the tears from my face. A distant sound of what was either a car door slamming or two birds colliding in the air awoke me.

I took one last moment of reflection, seeing the world through my father's eyes.

"I'm impressed," I thought.

"Hi, Impressed, I'm Dad."

32. ALASKA

Hey Bear, Don't Bother Me
Juneau, AK, September 19, 2015.

We stood in front of the Mendenhall Glacier Visitor Center in Juneau, Alaska, where three important things were about to happen. Next to me was my friend, Tin, who had agreed to go hiking with me.

It was my first new state in over a month. After Arizona, I spent four weeks in California, splitting time between Los Angeles and San Francisco, doing stand-up, a few speaking events, and mostly hanging out with my best friend, Nate. And thanks to my renewed vigor for my journey at the Grand Canyon, I also officially committed (to myself), for the first time, to be a nomad for at least a year. And if I wanted to complete all fifty states before I finished, that meant I had six months to do it.

Alaska was the first stop on my new itinerary because I assumed it was better to visit the northernmost state in the fall as opposed to winter when temperatures can hover in the negatives for months at a time. So I booked a speaking engagement, storytelling workshop, poetry show, and radio interview in Juneau and made my way to The Last Frontier.[64]

Tin, a friend of mine from P&G who lived in the Philippines, happened to be in the United States at the same time as my trip and decided to join me to see a climate very different from her own. And now we were there.

The first important thing that happened at the Visitor Center was I went

---

64 Not to be confused with the final frontier, which, as Captain Kirk has so clearly claimed, is space.

to the bathroom. That's not relevant to the story, but it is why we went into the Center to begin with, and at the time it was a particularly pressing matter.

The second important thing was that we saw some incredible sights through the telescopes they had set up inside the gift shop, including seeing two bald eagles perched on an iceberg floating in the middle of the water. Again, maybe not relevant, but it was pretty cool to see freedom sitting around.

The third, actually important thing happened when we approached the two rangers standing at the welcome kiosk in the Center.

"Hello, is there anything we can help you with?" the younger ranger asked as we approached.

The ranger who spoke was a young woman who appeared fresh out of college; the other was an older woman in her mid-fifties. Both were decked out in the muted green-and-brown uniform most rangers (that aren't of the Power variety) seemed to wear.

"Hello. We were hoping to do some hiking and wanted to see if you had any suggestions," Tin responded.

After some initial chit-chat about which trails we should do and where the best pictures were, one of the rangers nonchalantly struck fear in my heart.

"Oh, and you may see some black bears along the way; they're mostly harmless," the older ranger said, in the same manner you might say, "You may see some trees along the way."

I tried to appear cool about it, but inside I could already feel the anxiety building. Growing up in the suburbs in the Midwest, I never really had much interaction with wild animals. Mason, Ohio isn't exactly rife with nondomesticated creatures, unless you count newts, snakes, and fireflies (aka lightening bugs aka moon bugs aka fire devils aka golden sparklers aka blinkies). I had a feeling bears were way worse than any of those things.

"Really? Black bears you say? Are they dangerous?" I squeaked out.

"Not usually," Old Ranger replied. "Black bears are generally scared of humans. The only problem is if you are near one of their cubs."

"Right, of course, and what should we do if we see a bear?" I asked, ready to take down some of the most important notes I've ever transcribed.

"Black bears aren't like grizzly bears, so they'll run off if you make noise," Young Ranger said. My ageism came out as I began to wonder what a recent college grad could possibly know about the trials and tribulations of humanity and our inevitable mortality. "All you have to do is talk to it, and it'll go away," she continued as Old Ranger nodded in agreement.

Oh, so black bears are introverts. This weirdly comforted me, and my fear started to subside.

"Okay, but what do you say to the bear?" I asked. I didn't want to accidentally say the wrong thing and have the "mostly harmless" bear turn into a "very harmful to me" human destroyer.

The rangers both laughed. Young Ranger responded, "A lot of people just tell the bear what they're doing. 'Hello Mr. Bear, we're just walking on this trail. Don't mean to bother you.'"

I took a mental note, "So they prefer Mr. Bear over just Bear, and they don't have a PhD, so it's not Dr. Bear."

Old Ranger added, "Some people sing to the bear."

My fear started to return; they were clearly making fun of me. They were just making jokes and bears were really harbingers of death. "They sing to the bear? Now you're just messing with us," I replied.

More ranger laughter. "No really," Old Ranger said. "You just have to make noise to show the bear you aren't scared. There's even a song local kids sing."

Old Ranger cleared her throat before giving us her best rendition,

"In the summer, fall, and spring
The black bear sports and has his fling,
But winter sends him straight indoors and there he
Snores . . . and snores . . . and snores."

The fear once again waned, as I was convinced. Any bear scared by a diss track that lame is not one I'm afraid of. Plus, I didn't take Old Ranger as someone who could improvise a song on the spot, so I figured it must be a real thing. And if kids can handle a bear encounter, surely so could I.

"Thank you for the advice! We'll come back and let you know if we see any," Tin said, likely tired of me interrogating the rangers about an animal we probably wouldn't even see.

And with that, we headed off to the trail.

The hike was beautiful. There was a light rain nearly the entire trip—Juneau does sit in a rainforest after all—which just added to the naturey-ness of the whole thing. We got great pictures of Mendenhall Glacier in the background and hiked through the trees with views overlooking the surrounding area. We climbed our way up to AJ Falls where I took multiple selfies to add to my collection and enjoyed the afternoon.

Throughout it all, I thought exclusively of bears. At first, I hoped we wouldn't see one, that it was all much ado about nothing. But the more I thought about it, the more excited I became about the possibility of having my first bear encounter.

I started to think about what I would say to the bear. "Hey, Mr. Bear, what's going on? I'm just visiting all fifty states. How many have you been to? One? Bear, you gotta get out more."

Or, "Mr. Bear, wassssssaaaaaaaapppppppp? Hey, listen, we're just trying to explore nature so it would be awesome if you didn't, like, murder us. I want to get some pizza after this, not a tombstone."

As the hike continued, I thought maybe singing to the bear would be better, maybe something like Drake. "You know when that Hotline bling, that can only mean one thing." But then I worried that instead of leaving, the bear would start dancing, so I tried to remember the song the rangers sang.

"In the summer, fall, and spring
The black bear sports some kind of ring.
Something something something something,
And snores . . . and snores . . . and snores."

We hit the halfway point of the hike and started on the second half of the loop, a mostly downhill trek. I began to think that all my fear and preparation was for naught, that I would have no bear encounter and my songs would go to waste.

But then it happened.

As we made our way down a series of recently built wooden steps, fifteen yards in front of us was a black bear, chilling in the middle of the path. I immediately stopped. My heart began to race. This was the moment I had been fearing and then wanting and then preparing for.

I started to speak while also pulling out my phone to attempt a picture. I still hadn't decided between just talking to the bear or singing, so what came out was a horrible mash-up of the two:

"Hey bear, don't bother me.
And we will let you be.
But first, can we have,
A picture so we can show people we saw a bear, and they'll believe us."

Admittedly the song fell apart at the end, but it worked: the bear walked away. My preparation had paid off. I started off scared about that which I didn't understand, I did my research in talking with the rangers, and then through focus, practice, and resilience, I overcame my fears and persevered against all odds. It didn't matter that it wasn't a perfect song; it had worked.

And I had gotten a picture of it.[65]

    If you had told me at the beginning of my journey that I could success-fully fend off the meanest, baddest bear in the history of the entire universe with only my deep, bellowing voice, I wouldn't have believed you. But if you told me that now, after my trip to Alaska, I still probably wouldn't believe you. Because, if I'm being completely honest, I'm pretty sure Mr. Bear wasn't afraid of me, just annoyed. I swear, before he walked away, I saw him shake his head and mutter, "What an idiot."

---

65 You can see the blurry picture of the bear at tarv.in/alaska

Fun State Facts

Alaska has the highest bear population of the fifty states with an average of one bear for every twenty-one humans. Learning that made me think of other fun facts about the fifty states.

Alabama	Home to the world's only monument dedicated to an insect pest.
Alaska	Has the highest bear population, with one bear for every twenty-one humans.
Arizona	Known as "Nation's Valentine," because it joined the union on February 14.
Arkansas	The state instrument is the fiddle.
California	Largest producers of turkeys in the US.
Colorado	Issued the first license plate for a car in the US.
Connecticut	Is responsible for creating the telephone book.
Delaware	Was the last state to get a national park (in 2013).
Florida	Ponce de León landed there seeking the Fountain of Youth.
Georgia	Home to the largest drive-in fast food restaurant.
Hawaii	No building on Kauai can be built taller than a palm tree.
Idaho	Has an invented name with no meaning.
Illinois	Built the world's first modern skyscraper.
Indiana	Official state beverage is water.
Iowa	Only state that starts with two vowels.
Kansas	Where helium was discovered.
Kentucky	Contains a city built in a meteor crater (Middlesboro).
Louisiana	Only state that doesn't have counties.
Maine	Is the only one syllable state.
Maryland	Home to the first school in the US.
Massachusetts	Where the chocolate chip cookie was invented.
Michigan	Is shaped like a hand.
Minnesota	Inventions include snowmobile, water skis, stapler, and Bisquick.
Mississippi	Home to the International Checkers Hall of Fame.
Missouri	Name means "river of the big canoe."

Montana	Holds record for greatest temperature change in 24 hours (103°).
Nebraska	Originator of the 911 emergency system.
Nevada	Las Vegas has more hotel rooms than any other place on earth.
New Hampshire	Home to first potato grown in the US.
New Jersey	Is surrounded by water except for forty miles along NY border.
New Mexico	Santa Fe is the oldest capital city in the US.
New York	Jell-O, marshmallows, and gold teeth were all developed here.
North Carolina	Home to the first English colony (mysteriously just vanished one day).
North Dakota	Is the most rural of all US states.
Ohio	Birthplace of twenty-four astronauts and the Wright Brothers.
Oklahoma	The state flower is the mistletoe.
Oregon	The origin of its name is unknown.
Pennsylvania	Home to the first computer.
Rhode Island	Has the oldest running tavern in the US.
South Carolina	Contains towns named Coward, Due West, and South of the Border.
South Dakota	Has an annual Mashed Potato Wrestling Contest.
Tennessee	Graceland is the second most visited house in the country.
Texas	Six flags have flown over the state.
Utah	More Jell-O is eaten in Utah than anywhere else in the world.
Vermont	Has the only state capital that doesn't have a McDonald's
Virginia	Half of the US population lives within 500 miles of Richmond.
Washington	Only state to be named after a President.

Most facts from *Awesome America* (awesomeamerica.com).

33. ILLINOIS

Sick
Chicago, IL. September 28, 2015

This was a mistake. Not just going to Chicago, but going anywhere. The whole nomad thing was stupid, and I was stupid for doing it. What was the point? Why couldn't I live out of a house like a normal human being? Why did I do this to myself?

These were my thoughts as I curled up in the fetal position in a window seat on a Delta flight headed to O'Hare International Airport. I was nine days removed from my heroic actions in Alaska, and I felt like the world had flipped upside down, just like my stomach.

I was sick. On the road. And it sucked.

The first germ of sickness came after my last talk at the 2015 Applied Improvisation Network Conference in Montreal, Canada. I had flown there after my stay in Alaska and delivered two programs, including a TED-style talk on how improv has helped me break out of my shell and made me less socially awkward. According to some of my friends at the conference, it was one of the strongest talks I've ever delivered.

But as soon as the program ended and the conference was over, my immune system buckled under the weight of sleep-deprived nights, fun but stress-inducing talks, and hundreds of handshakes with people from twenty different countries harboring all manner of germs. By the time we had reached our cruising altitude on my flight, I had reached full-blown illness and miserability.

Originally, the plan was to enjoy some time in the Windy City before speaking at the University of Chicago on the 30th. I was going to eat at my favorite Chicago restaurants, Lou Malnati's and Portillo's, see some improv shows at iO, Second City, and CSz Chicago, and, best of all, reconnect with people.

According to Facebook—and that really seems to be the de facto source on these matters—I had more than sixty friends in the Chicago area, and this trip was meant to be a time to see many of them. I was going to meet up with fellow alumni from my improv group at Ohio State, catch up with old friends from high school, and check-in with former P&G colleagues. As it stood, I wasn't sure I would see any of those people ever again because I was fairly certain I was dying.

After what felt like an eternity (but was really less than three hours), the plane landed at ORD, and I made my way off the jet bridge. I found the nearest bathroom and introduced myself to John in a way more intimate than I'd like to discuss. After everything I had ever eaten was gone, I feebly washed up and made my way to customs. As I passed the line of passengers waiting to talk to border patrol, I thanked my lucky celestial beings that I had signed up for Global Entry and could breeze through immigration.

I shuffled to curbside pickup like a zombie man-child and waited. Instead of hopping on the "L" and heading downtown to crash at a friend's place like I was supposed to, I stepped on the first hotel shuttle that arrived. It took me to a nearby Super 8 motel; I got a room, and headed upstairs to suffer my illness alone. I dropped my two bags on the floor and crawled into bed with my shoes still on and my hoodie wrapped around me like a lonely man's hug.

The next thirty-six hours were a blur, a mix of sleeping, vomiting, and other gross things related to being sick. When I wasn't asleep or in the bathroom, I watched *Gotham* and ordered soup and crackers from a nearby restaurant on GrubHub. I repeated those activities on loop as if I was in a terrible version of *Groundhog's Day*, but instead of slowly learning from my mistakes, I just threw them up.

It was Arkansas all over again, but a thousand times worse. I was puking my guts out, miles from anyone and everything. Everything, that is, except my home. Because I didn't have one.

As I sat on the ground in the crappy motel bathroom, the disgusting tile floor cooling my hot skin, I thought about calling it quits, of ending the journey right then and there. I could cancel my talk at UChicago, book a flight to Ohio, and stay at my mom's forever. Or at least until I found my own place back in NYC, or LA, or wherever that wasn't a Super 8 motel.

My revelations in Arizona were all but forgotten; my resolve from Alaska was gone. The siren song of normalcy was calling, and I desperately wanted to answer. I wanted to return to a normal life where I had more than four shirts I could wear, owned more than three ounces of toothpaste, hair gel, and shampoo, and I didn't have to write down the room number of where I was staying because after countless nights on the road, the room number, hotel name, and city I was in were all starting to meld together.

I wanted to be done with the constant travel, and I could be. I could be done with all of the annoyances in Texas, the disappointments in Nebraska, and the challenges in Arkansas. I could be done with being sick in a hotel entirely by myself, with nothing but vending machine food and overpriced delivery services. I would still get sick, but I could do it in the comfort of my own home.

But as my fever and pity party reached their maximum vertex, I noticed something from where I was sitting on the bathroom floor. It was a tiny something in the bathtub. I looked closer. There, growing in the grout along the baseline of the tub, was a spot of mold. It should have grossed me out, but instead it reminded me of the trees from the Grand Canyon. I remembered the feeling of standing at Point Imperial, seeing the world around me.

I could be done. But, if I was done with the annoyances in Texas, I was also done with the hikes in Alaska. If I was through with the disappointments in Nebraska, I was also through with the pleasant surprises of Iowa. If I was over the challenges of Arkansas, I was over the rewards of Louisiana.

I thought back to my journey so far and everything I had learned, all the places I had seen, and all of the glorious food I had eaten. Nothing in life was without consequence, and if being sick on my own in a hotel room every now and then was the price I had to pay for these nomadic experiences, experiences like what I felt at the Grand Canyon, it was worth it.

Eventually, I crawled my way back into bed and slept. After a few more trips to the bathroom and the last few episodes of season one of *Gotham,* my fever dreams and lamentations receded. And as the fog of my sickness started to lift, so did my dire view of anything and everything.

By the third morning of being holed in up the motel, I was feeling well enough to leave and deliver the event for UChicago. I met up with one friend from P&G days and had one meal that wasn't soup: a burger and milkshake from Medici.

It wasn't my most exciting trip to Illinois. It wasn't as fun as performing at ComedySportz World Championships in the Quad Cities and wasn't as road trippy as visiting the World's Largest Golf Tee, Rocking Chair, and Knitting Needles in Casey. Previous and future trips to Chicago all led to more adventure. But none were as impactful.

As I checked out of the Super 8 motel on October 1, 2015, seven months after starting my journey, I knew, for the first time with 100 percent certainty, that I would accomplish my goal and that it would all be worth it.

34. OREGON

Salt & Straw and Ants
Portland, OR. October 4, 2015

Usually I hate lines, not the concept of connecting two points together, but standing in one.[66] But I was happy to be doing so now because it gave me time to make a decision.

I was in Portland, Oregon, suffering from the paradox of choice in the most delicious way possible. It was my first stop after being sick in Illinois, part of a two-state trip out West for shows and speaking events. I was with my good friend, Pat (not my former roommate but Pat from CSz), and he had brought me to Salt & Straw, an artisanal ice cream company with far too many eclectic choices.

Did I want one of their signature flavors, like Honey Lavender or Cinnamon Snickerdoodle? Or should I go with one of their Halloween flavors, like The Great Candycopia or A Potion of Malicious Delight?

"Any suggestions?" I asked Pat.

"They're all good," he replied, which was probably true, but not helpful.

We continued inching forward and made our way past the last bend in the queue. It would be my turn soon, and a tough decision was on the horizon. How could I possibly be expected to make a choice under such challenging circumstances?

---

66 For my fellow New Yorkers, no, it is not "standing on line." Rarely are you ever standing on any type of line, but you are always standing in a line. Plus you're in line with societal norms, not online like the internet.

I focused my listening to hear what other people were ordering. Maybe there would be something that people repeatedly requested, and that could help me make my decision.

Freckled Woodblock Chocolate. Sea Salt with Caramel Ribbons. Essence of Ghost.

At this point, it seemed like people were making up flavors, and they were getting served them. The line crept forward; the time of my decision was nigh and I didn't know what to do. In sales, they say, "a confused mind says no." It's just one consequence of the paradox of choice, the reality that we, as humans, get paralyzed by having too many options.

It's easy for us to pick between two things, A and B. We can compare and contrast, do a pros and cons list if we need to, or flip a coin. It's harder for us to decide between a lot of things, like A through Z. We try to compare A to B, B to C, C to D, and so on, the whole while we are trying to make the "right" choice.

We don't want to miss out on something that's incredible for something that's only good. We get paralyzed by all of the options, and instead of taking a risk and picking one, we take the easier route and pick none.

But I was not about to allow human flaws in processing prevent me from having ice cream. I decided that narrowing down flavors would be easier than selecting one from the entire menu, so I got to work. I removed anything from the board that sounded like it had fruit. Nothing against fruit, I'd just rather save that for when I'm pretending to be healthy, not when I'm eating dessert. Three flavors down.

Anything with nuts had to go, that's a midday snack, not an ice cream ingredient, and I prefer salt on fries, not ice cream. Two more gone. Coffee is disgusting, and alcohol is a drink, not an ingredient. Three more excluded.

It was down to eight final options:

~~Sea Salt with Caramel Ribbons~~	Double Fold Vanilla
~~Almond Brittle with Salted Ganache~~	Honey Lavender
Chocolate Gooey Brownie	Arbequina Olive Oil
~~Stumptown Coffee & Burnside Bourbon~~	~~Candy Corn~~
Cinnamon Snickerdoodle	The Great Candycopia
~~Strawberry Honey Balsamic w/ Black Pepper~~	~~Potion of Malicious Delight~~
~~Pear with Blue Cheese~~	~~Essence of Ghost~~
Freckled Woodblock Chocolate	Creepy Crawler Critters

I realized it was going to have to be a game-time decision; there was no way to choose based on the data I had. Maybe if I knew the monthly sales of each flavor, how long they had been around, or if I had more time I could do a text analysis on Foursquare reviews to see what flavors had the greatest frequency of mentions.

"Hi! Welcome to Salt & Straw. What can I get you?" the ice creamnista asked.

There was no time for analytics. "That's a good question," I responded. "This is my first time here, and I can't decide."

"Oh, well you're welcome to try as many flavors as you'd like."

I now understood why the line was not only long but also slow. I put my decision on hold, as it was time to gather more delicious data.

"Oh goodness," I said as if I were my grandmother. "Hmm, let me try the Honey Lavender and Snickerdoodle."

With two quick dips, I was given two tiny spoons of frozen dairy. I tried both and discarded the Honey I Shrunk the Spoons. They were both good but not quite what I was looking for.

"How about Olive Oil? And what is the Creepy Crawler?" I asked.

Another quick dip and I had Olive Oil. "The Creepy Crawler is matcha ice cream with candy bits topped with salted grasshopper and ant in crystal amber."

I laughed. The ice cream lady smiled. I stopped laughing. "Wait, are you serious? It has ants in it?"

"Yup," she replied.

I was appalled and curious at the same time. Ants were something I tried to keep off my food, not willingly put in it. At the same time, Salt & Straw was known for their quirky flavors and had been around awhile, so maybe they knew what they were doing.

"Okay . . . let me . . . try that?" the words came hesitantly.

One quick dip and I held a tiny spoonful of buggy ice cream. I looked at it, almost expecting to see the ants move or the grasshoppers hop. I saw neither as the bugs had been ground into hardened chocolate. I gave it a taste and made a face. The flavor was not for me. Not because of the bugs, I just don't think I like matcha.

"That was interesting," I offered. "I think I'll go with a small Chocolate Gooey Brownie."

"Coming right up."

Part of me knew all along that was the one I was going to get. It wasn't the most exotic flavor on the menu, but I like chocolate and brownies too much not to get ice cream with that as the name.

"Here you go," the scooperina said as she handed me a glorious cup of deliciousness.

As I took a taste of the delicious frozen treat, I felt a twinge of guilt. How dare I consider deciding what ice cream to eat a challenge? Complaining about having too many options was like complaining about having to travel. Compared to most circumstances, it was laughable to even consider it a problem. Some people were working hard just to put food, any food, on the table.

Admittedly, my challenge that night was toward the very end of the list of human predicaments, just above deciding what color ribbon to wrap around a present and below which Ikea dresser to buy. But, I conceded, it was still a (tiny, minuscule, not-that-big-a-deal) challenge.

And, no matter how small that challenge, I had prevailed. I had overcome a human limitation. I gathered data, made a decision, and was reaping the sweet reward. In a way, it was a microcosm of my nomadic journey. I was incredibility privileged even to be able to attempt what I was doing. I couldn't let one taste, one hard decision, or one three-day stint of being sick in a hotel room keep me from continuing.

Yes, I was definitely going to finish what I started: both the journey and this scoop of ice cream.

35. WASHINGTON

Uber Talkative in Washington
Seattle, WA. October 5, 2015

I stepped off the Amtrak train in Seattle and brought up the Uber app on my phone. I had thought about taking public transportation to get to my hotel, but I was tired and wanted nothing more than to get to my room and be by myself.

I had just spent the weekend in Portland, where I stayed with Pat and his family, as well as played in the ComedySportz show two nights before. It was an incredibly fun few days but had also drained my social battery, and I was ready to not be near anyone for a day.

I tapped REQUEST and waited for my Uber to arrive. Three minutes later, Francis showed up in his black Mazda, and I confirmed that his license plate matched the one on my phone. I had already made the mistake of getting into the wrong car once in New York; the child in the backseat was terrified.

I opened the door, confirmed he was Francis, and got in.

"Where you headed?" Francis asked. He was a bigger guy, with a gray bushy mustache in the shape of the top half of a football.

"Marriott Bellevue," I said succinctly, confused because I had put the destination into the app. I hoped he was more like the drivers in New York who barely speak to you, and less like the drivers in Ohio who talk from the moment the door opens to the moment you open it again to leave. His opening question didn't bode well.

"Ah, it's good to get out of downtown," he replied. "There's a Seahawks game today."

"That's good. Hopefully, we don't hit traffic," I responded while staring out the window.

"It should be fine. You a Seahawks fan?"

"Cincinnati Bengals."

"Ooh, the Bengals are looking good this year. You might finally win a playoff game."

"Yep."[67]

"I'm a Seahawks fan," Francis shared, "since before they were good. I still remember when they played in the Kingdome, and they were terrible. They went ten years without making the playoffs. That was back when they were in the AFC. Did you know that? They started in the NFC, got moved to the AFC, and then went back to the NFC. It was crazy. Then that rich guy from Microsoft bought 'em, brought in Holmgren, and things got better. They moved to the new stadium and went to the Super Bowl only to be robbed by the refs against the Steelers. It was a conspiracy. The powers that be didn't want the Seahawks to win. Then of course now we have the Super Bowl Champion Seahawks led by Carroll. Did you know he's the oldest coach in the league? He doesn't look like it. It's like he found the Fountain of Youth or something."[68]

There was the briefest of silence before he continued, "What brings you to Seattle?"

He asked me a question, so I had to respond. "I'm doing some work with Microsoft. You?"

"I live here. What type of work?"

(Conversation deferment failed.)

"Corporate training. We're working with recent hires on how they're showing up."

"How they're showing up? Like coming in late?" he asked.

"No, like how they do their work. Some Type-A people do a good job of getting results, but they leave a trail of destruction behind them making it harder to advance later. We teach them how they do something is just as important as what they do."

"Oh. How do you do that?"

"Well, this particular training is two days that covers things like their long-term goals, personal brand, and how to leverage their jobs to get what

---

67 Note: the Bengals did not win a playoff game that year but rather lost to the Steelers in very Bengals fashion, blowing a lead in the final minutes thanks to a fumble and some very dumb penalties. The loss extended their streak of twenty-five seasons without a playoff win.

68 I have no idea if this is what he actually said because, to be perfectly honest, I wasn't listening, instead dreaming of the solitude that would come with getting to my hotel room.

they want out of life."

"That's cool."

"Thanks." I stared out the window. It was a beautiful day in Seattle, no mistiness to be found. The sun peeked from behind some clouds as we drove across the I-90 floating bridge. The gentle hum of the car riding smoothly along the road created a great environment to daydream. Sadly, Francis did not.

"Can I ask you a question," Francis asked, breaking the peaceful silence with his slightly accented voice.

My eyes met his through the rearview mirror. I hoped my face didn't betray my unhappiness for being pulled away from my moment of solitude, but I don't think it would have mattered anyway.

I wasn't mad at Francis for wanting to talk. I'm sure, as a driver, there were long stretches of time when he didn't talk to anyone. And though my trip would only last about twenty minutes, he would be driving all day, and conversation was one of the only distractions he had.

I understood why he wanted to talk; I just didn't want to. I had spent the whole weekend around people and was about to spend the next two days leading an event for nearly a hundred others. I wanted to go to my hotel room, get food from Din Tai Fung Dumpling House, and waste a few hours on Reddit. I needed that time to recharge. It was how I functioned as an introvert in a profession that is almost nothing but talking to other people.

Being an introvert doesn't mean I hate people; I love what I do. I love speaking, training, coaching, and have even grown to like the networking that comes with it all. It just means it takes energy for me to do it and that I need time on my own to get re-energized. Which is why, as great as ridesharing services like Uber and Lyft are,[69] I feel like they're missing a critical feature: an introversion scale.

When ordering a ride, I should be able to select how much I want the driver to talk to me. On one side, there would be an E (for Extrovert), and it means, "Let's become best friends in this thirteen-minute trip to 74th and Amsterdam." On the other side would be I (for Introvert) which means, "Don't even say hello; just nod as I get in, and let's sit in the beautiful sounds of silence on our hour drive to JFK."

It would be a scale, how Introversion and Extroversion are in real life, and you would select before each trip. Because no matter who you are, sometimes you feel like being chatty, and other times you just want to be left on your own, like I yearned for in that very moment.

---

69 If you don't know what Uber and Lyft are, it's like Airbnb but for driving. If you're still confused, grab the nearest millennial and have them explain the internet.

But, with no mute button to push, I responded reluctantly to Francis's question, "Sure."

And for the remainder of the trip, we talked about some of the content I'd be training and about how he could use Uber to help finance some of the other things he wanted to do in life. Being a good coach for someone doesn't require expertise in what that person does; it just requires listening well, asking questions, and sharing perspective. So that's what I did: listened, asked questions, and shared perspective.

Before long, we got to the hotel, and Francis thanked me for the advice. Though it wasn't quite the drive I was hoping for, I was happy to share some ideas that might give him some guidance. Francis was a kindhearted person, eager to help people, and excited to do new things. He didn't have the easiest life but was making great strides to do things better.

Our conversation reminded me that, despite the fact I was on my own so often, not everything was about me or what I wanted. Sometimes, it was about what other people needed. Instead of being focused on my own selfishness, I should think about how I could help other people, even when I'm tired or drained. Even though I was the one providing the coaching, it was really Francis teaching the lesson.

"Go Hawks," I said as I shut the door and he drove off. I pulled out my phone, and Uber asked for a rating. We had had a great conversation, but he sure did talk a lot. Four Stars.

36. INDIANA

Dreams of Gratitude
Indianapolis, IN. October 8, 2015

I knocked on the door and waited. I wasn't nervous, per se, but the first time you sleep on a friend's couch is always a little nerve-wracking. You don't know what their apartment will be like, how much they'll want to talk, how comfortable their couch/spare bed/beanbag chair will be, and whether or not the friend you've known for years is secretly a hoarder.

I was in Indianapolis, Indiana, and was about to find out how a good friend lived. After Washington, I had flown to Ohio for a keynote event and then driven to Indianapolis for a ComedySportz show and stand-up set. In the morning, I'd drive back to Ohio for a day before heading to New York. For the night, I'd be staying with the man we all referred to by last name, Colby.

Colby and I met years before through CSz. We had performed together multiple times and had shared a stage kiss that is forever immortalized in a picture on Facebook, so it was fitting that my time in Indianapolis included performing in another show with him and platonically sleeping on his couch.

A few seconds after knocking, I heard footsteps approach the door and prepared myself for the intimate moment of entering another human's docking station.

"Drewski," Colby said as he opened the door.

"Colby," I replied, matching his tone and voice.

"Come on in!"

I accepted his offer and crossed the threshold into his abode.[70] Immediately, I felt comfortable. The place was clean, the mood was light, and best of all, there was no topography of fast food trash creating a mountain range of garbage in his living room.

"You can set your bags down here, and I'll give you a quick tour," Colby said.

I set my bags down as he talked.

"This is the living room, it's used for living. That's the dining area, for dining. In there is the kitchen for kitching, and down the hall, you have rooms for beds and baths."

I took a mental note of where the room with the bath was located.

"And this is the best thing in the entire apartment," Colby continued as he put his arms on the shoulders of his fiancé at the time but now turned wife, Kaitlyn.

"Hi, Kaitlyn," I said. "It's great to see you again. I agree with Colby. You're probably the best thing here."

She smiled, "Thanks, Drew."

"Can I get you anything?" Colby asked.

"I think I'm good for now," I responded, "I'll probably grab some water in a bit."

"Make yourself at home. The water is some of the best the city of Indianapolis has to offer," Colby replied.

I sat down on the couch as highlights from that night's Indianapolis Colts win played on TV, and the three of us chatted. We reminisced about old times, caught up on the present, and made a week's worth of jokes.

Colby: "No, these aren't skinny jeans. I'm just gaining weight."
Me: "Whenever I dream about horses I have night mares."
Colby: "Don't forget the mushrooms when cooking. That's the morel of the story."
Me: "If I had to estimate the number of fist bumps I've given in my life, I'd say a ton. As in 2,000 pounds."
Colby: "You're so stupid, and I love it."

And that was our night. Conversation and laughs, three friends catching up. The fact I also had somewhere to sleep was an added bonus. After just the right amount of talking, and as the clock approached midnight, we all decided it was time to go to sleep. Kaitlyn said goodbye and headed home; Colby and

---

70 Vampires aren't the only ones who wait to be invited into a home; we with good manners do it as well.

I prepped for bed.

"Let me show where you're sleeping." He spread his arms wide in front of the couch and said, "Tada!"

"It's perfect," I replied. Pretty much anything that wasn't sleeping in a car was perfect at this point.

"Here's a sheet you can lay down, a comfy pillow for your soft head, and a blanket for warmth and safety from monsters."

"Thanks," I said, turning the comfortable couch into my makeshift bed for the night.

Colby headed to his room and, as I laid me down to sleep, I thought about how fortunate I was to have such an incredible network of friends. Not only did they make the journey possible by letting me crash on their couch, they made it worthwhile.[71]

Reconnecting with people all around the world was often a highlight of each destination. Like the countless times I stayed with Brady, Ian, and Matt in NYC and got to hear about the strides they were each making in the comedy world. Or when Tamara and I would swap stories of where we had recently traveled, or when Chris and I reflected on our time at Ohio State.

Friends like Raman provided me with encouragement and ideas for even doing such a trip. My best friend Nate kept me sane throughout the whole thing and offered a place to stay whenever I was in LA. Christopher helped me gain perspective on my journey. People like Jaclynn acted as a tour guide for me to see their city. Courtney gave me recommendations for where to eat, Lauren took me to get incredible gelato, Pat kept me grounded in the funniest ways possible, and Rachel gave me a place to call home even when I was without one.

The intimacy of the arrangements also led to more meaningful conversations. It's one thing to meet a friend to catch up over coffee; it's another to have that chat while in your pajamas sitting on their couch. In total, twenty-six friends let me stay at their place, none of them charging me a dime for it (or any other amounts of money for that matter). That was the best part about staying with friends. It wasn't that it cost me nothing more than conversation—which admittedly is a cost for an introvert—it was that it gave me a chance to reconnect with old acquaintances for auld lang syne.

Eventually, my thoughts of gratitude turned to dreams of rainbows and milkshakes, and I slept.

In the morning, Colby was up before I was. He had set out a towel for

---

71 Not literally crash on their couch. Sometimes I delicately sat on it. Other times it wasn't a couch, but a sofa or loveseat. Sometimes it was an extra bed (those were the best). Once it was a beanbag chair.

me to use and offered me breakfast. We chatted some more and then left his apartment together.

"Hey Colby," I said as we opened our respective car doors. "Thanks for letting me crash here. I hope I wasn't like a jockey and *saddled* you with too much work."

He groaned before smiling. "Of course, man, anytime."

It was the nice thing to say, which is no surprise considering he's one of the nicest people on the planet. The crazy thing is that he truly meant it.

"Oh, and should I stop making horse puns?" I asked.

Colby thought for a second and then smiled. "I say, 'neigh.'"

Tips for Letting Me Stay at Your Place

While twenty-six people letting me crash at their place may seem like a lot, it's really less than 0.01 percent of the entire adult population in the United States. So, in a way, it's quite a privilege to have me sleep at your house. As such, I've put together some tips for letting me stay at your place.

1. **Post the Wi-Fi information somewhere.** The most basic need you can provide me with while I'm staying with you is Wi-Fi, especially if you live in an area with a poor cellphone signal. Chances are I'm also going to want to connect more than one device, so verbally telling me the information is okay, but it's even better to have it posted somewhere, especially if you never took the time to update your SSID or password and I have to connect to B0DECDG with passcode 15L0LSDTH1$1$m4duP1WTF.

2. **Let me know where the most accessible plug is.** Number two behind Wi-Fi is electricity as it seems like my phone is always about to die. Ideally, you would have a plug or an extension cord right next to where I'm going to sleep, but at a minimum, help me out with the best spot to plug in my phone if it's not super obvious.

3. **Keep a hand towel in the bathroom.** The worst part of any bathroom experience is washing your hands only to find there's no towel on which to dry them. Then you have to shake them off and wipe them on your pants or a nearby couch, and that's more work and less efficient. Plus, if you don't have a towel in your bathroom, it makes me wonder if you ever wash your hands since you don't seem to be in need of drying them.

4. **Also, put a wastebin in there.** Not everything that happens in a bathroom can or should be flushed. If I want to break all the rules and use a Q-Tip to clean my ears, or should I have to blow my nose, I don't want to waste more water with a flush when it could easily go into a garbage can.

5. **Have bar soap.** I understand that you might use liquid soap and a loofa when you shower, but that creates a problem for your guests. Do you want us to use your loofa as well? I didn't think so. A bar of soap helps us both avoid an awkward sharing of skin cells.

6. **Have a nightlight.** I don't know the layout of your home, so if I get up in the middle of the night, it's helpful if there's a little light to guide me to the bathroom or kitchen, lest I wake you up from screaming while I fall down the stairs.

7. **Tell me about anything that might be creepy.** Every place has its eccentricities, particularly some that may frighten unaware guests. Does the wind sometimes cause a branch to hit a nearby window? Does the radiator hiss and pop throughout the night? Is there a ghost that sometimes inhabits people as a vessel in the astral plane to murder those who slumber within its realm? A warning would be nice.

8. **Let me know of any house rules up top.** Hey, it's your house, and they're your rules. Just let me know what they are, so I don't accidentally violate them. Is yours a take-off-your-shoes house? No problem; just let me know. Do you prefer windows open instead of AC on? Give me some heads up. Do you play Farmer's Hand in Euchre? Tell me before the game starts, so you can't pull one over on me.

9. **Along the same lines, let me know of any pet peeves.** I get it: we all have our preferences when it comes to the way things are done, and I don't want to annoy you while I'm there. If you're particular about how dishes are cleaned or blankets are folded, the only way I'll know is if you tell me. Otherwise, you'll be getting all your bedding in one stack of imperfect rectangles at the end of the couch.

10. **Don't be afraid to ask for my help.** I'm staying at your place for free, so it's okay for you to ask me to help with a task that requires my skillset, such as needing a second pair of hands to help hang a picture, longer arms to replace a light bulb, or a handsome face for you to work on your portrait painting skills. Just make sure the task can be done in a relatively short amount of time and doesn't make me wish I had shelled out for a hotel room.

By following these simple tips, you too could be lucky enough to let me crash on your couch.

37. CONNECTICUT

The Days Are Just Packed
Meriden, CT. October 13, 2015

The best gift I've ever received was the gift of life. I don't mean that I have a kid, I mean my own life. Without it, any other gifts would be a waste on nothingness.

The second-best gift was *The Complete Calvin and Hobbes* [Box Set], a fourteen-pound collection of every *Calvin and Hobbes* cartoon strip by Bill Watterson. My mom got it for me for my twenty-somethingth birthday, and it is phenomenal.

Growing up, I loved reading the comics in the newspaper, and *Calvin & Hobbes* was the best. I enjoyed the incredible artwork and the funny predicaments Calvin found himself in. Rereading the cartoon as an adult, I appreciated the deep life lessons Watterson elegantly shared through the panes.

So it was with delight that I hiked Guiffrida Park in Meriden, Connecticut, during the middle of the day on a Tuesday in October with Rachel because I felt as if I was in a *Calvin & Hobbes* strip. Rachel was Hobbes, the more grounded, level-headed, sarcastic one of the two of us. I was Calvin, pontificating about things I didn't really understand and making rash decisions in the name of adventure.

I was back in the Northeast for a few days and was delivering an event later that evening in a town nearby. Rachel had the day off from her physical therapy program at Columbia, so we decided to spend the afternoon enjoying the beauty that was the Northeast in the fall.

The scene was as picturesque as Bill Watterson might have drawn it in the Sunday, full-color spread. All around us, leaves were exhibiting their colorful hues, creating a forest of red, orange, and yellow for us to explore. The air was crisp; the temperature hovering right around "oh, it's a bit nippy out."

As we started our hike, I imagined myself as Calvin during one of his lazy summer days. I bounced around from rock to rock, taking pictures and talking philosophically.

"Do you think everything happens for a reason?" I asked Rachel.

"Why, what did you do?" She responded perfectly as Hobbes.

"What? Nothing. I mean in general, like do you think we met for a *reason?*" I said doing air quotes.

"Well, yeah," she replied. "The reason was that I went to your show, and we all went for drinks afterward. So was there a reason we met? Yes. But was there a reason in some cosmic sense; that's harder to say."

"That's what I mean," I said. "Like people always say, 'everything happens for a reason.' But I feel like that 'reason' is often just chance or luck, or because you did something good, or maybe something dumb. Like the reason we met was really just chance."

Rachel was quiet, either displeased with my answer or distracted by our current view. We had made our way to the peak of the trail where we could see a tapestry of colors stretched before us as far as the human eye without any cybernetic enhancements could see. The view, combined with the fact we had just been hiking, made the experience figuratively and literally breathtaking.

"So, you don't think that it was fate?" she eventually asked.

I looked at Rachel and smiled. "I don't think it was fate. I think it was circumstance." I reached out and gave her a hug. "I think it was very fortunate circumstance. I'm happy I met you, but I don't think it was necessarily 'destined to happen.' I'm sorry if that's not romantic."

She pushed me away. "You don't think we're soulmates?"

Her lips appeared to reveal a slight grin, but I wasn't sure. I didn't know if she was upset about the conversation or messing with me. She turned and continued our walk along the edge of the overlook.

"I don't really believe in soulmates," I finally said.

She stopped to raise her eyebrows at me. Maybe she was upset after all.

"Let me explain," I tried. "I don't think 'soulmates' exist, at least not in the traditional sense. I mean I'm an engineer; I'm not entirely convinced that souls exist. But the idea that there is only one person out there, out of seven billion on our planet, who you're meant to be with? That's crazy to me. What if you only had one shot to meet that person and you missed it, like B. Rabbit at the beginning of *8 Mile?*"

She shook her head at my reference.

I continued, "But that suggests that we all have our individual destinies, which I don't believe. Destiny and fate remove choice from the equation. If I was destined to meet you, then I wasn't in control and therefore not responsible for my actions leading up to our being together. It wasn't that I chose to flirt with you at the bar after my show; it was that destiny preordained it. Or since then, it's not you who sacrificed so much for us to be together while I travel; it's just all part of a larger plan."

This last part was particularly true for her. Rachel and I had met a few months before I became a nomad. The relationship was still new, and I didn't know what life on the road would be like, so we stayed in contact. We would grab dinner when I was in town, but we weren't together. Eventually, in September, I realized I wanted to be with her even while I was traveling and asked her to be my girlfriend. She said yes, despite knowing I'd be on the road for at least five more months, because she was a kind and patient person who also happened to be really busy with school at the moment.

As we started our descent back to the car, she remained silent, not betraying how she felt about what I was saying. So I kept rambling.

"And if that's true for love, then it's true for everything. It's like when people say 'everything happens for a reason,' or worse, 'everything happens for the best.' No, it doesn't. Tell people who got into a car accident and can no longer walk that everything happens for the best. Or tell it to the parents who lost their kid to leukemia, or the thousands of infants born into poverty every single day. Life isn't fair. But it's also not unfair. It just is. Life happens, and there's no puppet master pulling the strings behind it. There's just chaos, circumstance, and choice."

The day's strip had taken a deeper turn from the playful Calvin whence it began, so I dove deeper.

"I think people mistake that choice for fate. People see someone who has overcome incredible circumstances to achieve success, and they say 'see, that bad thing happened for a reason.' No, that bad thing happened, and that person chose to make it into something. They decided to turn their paralysis into a career as an inspirational speaker or their lost daughter into a nonprofit to provide support for families battling cancer."

Rachel and I reached another overlook. I was nearing the conclusion of my thoughts, so I couldn't stop now.

"All of that to say, I don't believe in soulmates. I think there are multiple people out there who you can be compatible with, and ultimately, it's up to two people to mutually decide that they want to be together. I don't think love is some mysterious thing that comes from fate but rather a combination of chaos, circumstance, and choice. And people who are happy long term are people who make a choice to stay together. They aren't obsessed with finding their 'one true love' and don't mistake the gradual decline of romantic love as a sign things have to end. Instead, they both decide they want it to work with that person instead of a player to be named later. And isn't that kind of romantic in and of itself? Two people choosing to be together despite all of the other chaos around them?"

Rachel looked at me blankly for what felt like an eternity. Then she flashed a smile before leaning in and giving me a kiss on my cheek. "I agreed with you the whole time. I don't believe in soulmates or fate or destiny or any of that stuff, either. I just wanted to mess with you. I mean that was quite the loop you took to get there. Did you really bring up leukemia?"

"I mean . . ." I stumbled.

"I'm just kidding. It was kinda cute in a morbid way, but I understand what you were saying. I think it's a choice, too."

I relaxed and let out a sigh before smiling. Rachel was more like Hobbes than I thought.[72]

---

72 I realize this metaphor isn't perfect as Calvin and Hobbes were never romantic with each other. Also Hobbes was a stuffed tiger for everyone but Calvin. I assure you that Rachel is a real person.

38. NEW JERSEY

Whatever Floats Your Boat
Hoboken, NJ. October 16, 2015

The wind off the Hudson River tousled my hair from its gel-laden place. I looked over at Rachel, her longer locks going just about everywhere. She wasn't happy.

We were on the New Jersey Ferry headed to Hoboken, and I was taking us to the Garden State, so I could perform in a show and add it to my list. She was gracious about it as usual, but it wasn't the Friday evening she had envisioned when I had suggested we have a night out together.

Originally the plan was dinner at a nice restaurant in Manhattan followed by sipping cocktails at a jazz club. And then I learned about a poetry show in NJ that I could perform at and the evening went from "nice date with Rachel" to "I'm going to perform; come if you want."

Under normal circumstances, she'd be happy to go with me to check off another state (like in Connecticut), but we had agreed to one plan, and I had changed everything last minute without even asking her. It was an unfair date-and-switch.

I was hoping that taking the ferry would be fun, and I could pass it off as a romantic start to our evening: Rachel and I would feel the cool breeze as we looked up at the stars while holding hands at the stern of the boat. We'd laugh, we'd smile, we might even make out.

Instead, the wind was aggressively cold, the stars were covered by clouds, and the only hand I was holding was my own as I tried to keep it warm with my hot breath. It didn't help that I insisted we stay up top to see what I hoped would be a romcom-esque view rather than sit inside where there was plenty of heat and zero wind.

It began to sink in why Rachel wasn't swept away by my last-minute change of plans. I was only in town for a couple more days before I was off to my next state, and I had chosen to perform on our last completely free night without asking if she was okay with that. We weren't going on a date so much as checking off a place on my travel list, and our boat ride wasn't a romantic way to see the city; it was public transportation.

I had been a nomad for so long, on my own so often, that I forgot not everything was about me. If Rachel and I were together, it meant I had to be comfortable with us making decisions together. I couldn't just do what I wanted at the spur of the moment, not if it also affected her. This wasn't a bad thing, just something I wasn't used to during my journey.

I hugged Rachel for warmth and apologized.

"I'm sorry I turned our date night into an errand. We don't have to do the show if you don't want to. I'd rather us hang out and have a good time."

She didn't say anything, possibly because she didn't want to rub it in that I had been a goober—or because I was muffling her speech in my attempt to keep us both warm. She eventually murmured, "It's okay."

As we knotted our way further from New York, the mood started shifting. It was a slow shift, like the vessel beneath us, but it was a shift. The gentle sound of the water around us was soothing, and the lights from the cities on either side reflected off the water.

I rocked her back and forth in my arms, feeling like a kid, hoping that my apology would patch things up. I attempted to make terrible jokes to get her to laugh.

"If this boat were in a Disney movie, would it have a ferry godmother?"
"If something goes wrong, don't blame me. Ship happens."
"Look, that water marker is doing such a good job. Yeah, bouyyyyyyy!"

They were moderately successful, not because they were good but because they were so bad. And with each passing moment, the mood lightened, and the experience became more romantic.

We forgot about the cold (or had become numb to it) and took in our surroundings. We turned to look at the incredible NYC skyline, illuminating the dark sky with its bright lights that will inspire you, the concrete jungle where dreams are made of, and other Alicia Keys lyrics.

The night was indicative of how I felt about New Jersey in general. I've never been particularly ecstatic about heading there. It's an annoying place to drive: you have to pay a toll any time you want to leave, you're not allowed to pump your own gas, and they seemed to be against left turns, forcing you to do those weird jug-handle roundamajigs. But, like every state in the union, it had some incredibly nice people, passionate and talented performers, and beautiful views, even if many of those views were of New York. I've enjoyed many a trip to the state once I let go of any preconceived notions about the place and learned to enjoy the moment for what it was.

I spun us around so that we could see the Jersey side. It wasn't as majestic as the view behind us, but it was where we were headed. We were supposed to have a romantic date night in the city that never sleeps, but instead, we were headed to "Mile Square City," and we were already across the Hudson. It was time to focus on the future.

In the end, we would have a fun evening. We'd grab some moderately-delicious pizza in downtown Hoboken before heading to bwe kafe where we would enjoy a poetry show and a chocolate frappe. My reading would go well, and we'd end our New Jersey adventure with a cupcake and train ride back to Rachel's.

I squeezed her a little tighter. Despite my denseness and the stereotypes of Jersey, on that night it was the setting for a romantic evening. Eventually.

39. KENTUCKY

Life Stages
Covington, KY. October 25, 2015

It was a perfect Midwestern Sunday. After getting through some work and exercising at my mom's place in Ohio, I headed south to Kentucky to see my good friend, Phil. We had a busy day of watching football, playing video games, and just relaxing on the calendar. I was back in the Midwest for a couple of speaking engagements and to finally check off the Bluegrass State.

I pulled up to a house in the small town of Covington, Kentucky, located just across the river from Cincinnati.[73] It was the home of Devou Park, has some of the best views of the Cincinnati skyline, is the reason that the Cincinnati airport—which is located in Kentucky—is called CVG, and was the new residence of Phil and his family.

Phil and I first met in New York, but he had recently moved back to the Tri-State area (OH-KY-IN) with his wife, Heather, their dog and cat, and in the near-future, baby Theo. We had only been friends for a few years, but it always felt like we had known each other our whole lives. Maybe it was because we grew up near each other, had some of the same mutual friends, and had both been long-suffering Cincinnati Bengals fans. Or maybe it was our shared love for doing really stupid things in GTA 5. Whatever it was, we had connected quickly, and I was excited to catch up with him.

---

73 I say "small town" but Covington is technically a city with a population of 40,000 people. That's good enough to be the fifth largest city in Kentucky. For comparison, that wouldn't even crack the Top 25 for Ohio.

I grabbed my game day snacks from the trunk and knocked on the door of his home.

"Well look who finally made it to Kentucky," Phil said as he opened the door, a huge smile on his face.

Looking at the size of his place, I replied, "Well look who made it in Kentucky; this place is huge!"

He laughed and welcomed me in. I set my bags of chips and dips on the counter, and he gave me a tour. The place was incredible. It was three stories tall, each floor with high ceilings. One floor alone was bigger than either of our respective places when we were in New York. His bathroom had more open space than most NYC bedrooms, and his closet space rivaled the size of the boutiques in SoHo. I had forgotten just how much space you could get if you decided not to live on a twenty-two-square-mile island with two million other people.

The place was still lightly decorated, a function of the move being somewhat recent, but was already filling out into a home. The previous owner had installed a number of things like shelves and showerheads meant for a man 6'0" or taller, which was perfect for Heather, who stands at 5'2". But that was okay because Phil could change anything he wanted because he didn't have to worry about returning a security deposit: the dude was a homeowner.

"Wow, that shower head is really high," I commented as he showed me one of the bathrooms.

"Yeah," Phil replied, "When you shower, it feels like you're cleaning yourself in the rain. It's fun."

The shower itself was large enough to re-enact scenes from *Singing in the Rain* if you wanted to, so I imagined it was fun indeed.

The tour ended back in his living room where we sat and watched football on a 50" flat-screen TV. We ate Skyline Chili Dip (one of the greatest things you can ever put in your mouth) and drank from a collection of beverages Phil had stocked in his massive refrigerator. And we caught up.

"So how is life on the road?" Phil asked.

"It's good," I replied. "I've decided I'm definitely doing it for a year and hitting all of the states."

"Ah, so that's why you came across the river to Kentucky."

"I mean that's not the only reason I came to Kentucky. I wanted to see your place and eat your food."

"Well we've got plenty of it, so have at it. Have you figured out what you're going to do when you stop being a nomad?" he asked.

"I haven't really thought about it yet," I said because I hadn't really thought about it yet. There was still so much thinking and planning to do to get through the next few months, to hit the last eleven states, and to complete my selfie collection.

"Rachel's open to leaving New York," I continued, "and I'm still considering a move to the West Coast for warmer weather, so we'll see."

"Well, you could always move back here," Phil said. "I've already shown you that there are some great restaurants popping up."

That was true. The last time I was in town, Phil planned a night for me, him, Heather, and my mom, to have delicious fried chicken at The Eagle followed by donuts at Holtman's. It was his not-so-subtle way to say, "Hey, you can get your favorite foods here, too. They're still delicious and a lot cheaper."

"Plus you get more space, everything is less expensive, and you can buy Pop Tarts in bulk at Costco," Phil piled on. "And you could play soccer again at Tri-County Sportsplex," he added, lilting his voice at the end.

He was right; I could have this. I could have what Phil had, or I could at least try to model what he had created so well. He was married to an incredibly awesome woman, owned a spectacular home, and had a little one on the way. He worked a job he enjoyed and lived close to both his and Heather's parents. He played video games when he had the time, watched football on the weekends, and knew where he was resting his head every single night.

He was living the American Dream. Or, rather, an American Dream. He had a house, a car, and a family. He didn't have a white picket fence though; his was brown.

But as incredible as it all was, it wasn't my dream. At least not yet. My dream included finishing the fifty states, continuing to build a business that helped people every single day, improving myself as a speaker, comedian, and person, finding ways to be more efficient, and eating like a twelve-year-old (in moderation of course).

And that's the thing about life. What success looks like for me is different than what it is for Phil, or for Beyoncé, or that lady over there, or a cat or a dog or an ant or an aunt. What is success to me—traveling around, working with organizations, performing—might be abhorrent to others. Depending on whom you asked, I was either a self-employed, location independent, humor consultant or an unemployed, homeless man-child.

It was like the video games we would soon start playing. I was Assassin's Creed, bouncing around from spot to spot, hopefully having a quick impact, and then moving on. Phil was Destiny, building something sustainable long-term and improving every step of the way. We were both heroes with incredible skills and really cool outfits.

He and I were just at different stages in different games. He might look at me and envy that I've built my own business just as I might look at him and envy the life he had with his family. But neither of us was jealous; we were happy for one another. We were both successful by our own standards.

"Maybe," I eventually replied, "but I'm not sure I'm there yet."

We took a break from watching football and picked up the controllers for his X-Box. We were both playing the game of life, he was just playing *Phil,* and I was working on the levels of *Drew.*

40. NEW YORK

Running to a Marathon
New York, NY. November 1, 2015

I sprinted my way down 73rd Street. My lungs burned with the cold November air. My legs grew tired, and I wanted to stop, to collapse on the ground and sleep for a week. But we were close to the finish, and I couldn't give up now. I powered through the doubt and the pain.

I wasn't running the New York Marathon, but I was running to watch it, and Rachel and I were running late. I was back in New York City for a few days after my visit to Kentucky and a short hop to Canada. We were meeting up with friends and didn't want to miss seeing Vinnie run by. Eventually, we made it through the mass of people to find a group of enthusiastic fans wearing custom-made "Run Vinnie Run" t-shirts.

The scene, like it is every year, was boisterous and positive. People lined the streets to support their friends, family, and fellow humans. People cheered from balconies above, like you would kids in a third grade play or the dogs during Puppy Bowl. A rock band played on the doorstep of a nearby bar to provide a soundtrack on the run. Throngs of strangers yelled out people's names if they were written on their shirt; in lieu of names, they yelled out what color shirt they were wearing, "Go blue shirt! Run!" or sometimes their number, "You can do it 1–2–2–6–0!"

Those closest to the runners held up their hands for high fives and fist bumps. There was hootin' and hollerin,' clapping and cheering, and I'm sure some posh British person saying, "I say, what a mighty fine effort these blokes are making."

People carried signs to share individual messages of encouragement to their loved ones. "You can do it, Sheryl; we're proud of you!" and "Go, David! You got this! Note: This sign is for David S., but if you're also named David, go you!"

Others had signs just to make people laugh, like "WORST PARADE EVER," "WHERE IS EVERYONE GOING?" and my favorite, "SHAKE SHACK IS ONLY 10 BLOCKS PAST THE FINISH LINE."

Nearly 50,000 people would complete the marathon that day, with an estimated 2 million people lining up to watch it happen in person and another 300 million watching the event on TV. That's forty live supporters for every one runner.

In between the yelling and cheering, I thought about how crazy the whole thing was. First, for people to say, "Yes, I want to run 26.2 miles" is insanity by itself. We've developed better modes of transportation since Philippedes first carried the message from Marathon to Athens, not to mention technology like cellphones and texts. Plus, can we all agree that honoring that first marathon is a little weird to begin with? Do you know why he ran 26.2 miles? To announce the Greeks had beaten the Persians in battle. He was running to gloat. I can understand the urgency if you lost the battle and had to warn the town of an impending attack, but to run all that way just to be like, "We're #1?" And, what most people forget, is that as soon as Philippedes shared the message, he dropped dead. And people are like, "Yeah, I'm going to do that, too; it sounds like a fun Sunday."

But people not only run it, millions of others come out and support them in their crazy goal to push themselves physically and mentally.

There, in the middle of hundreds of screaming supporters, I grew hopeful for humanity. So often we hear all about the things that divide us: Republican vs. Democrat, Introvert vs. Extrovert, Ohioan vs. Michigander. But we don't always talk about the things that bring us together.

Things like cheering each other on. This type of support happens on smaller scales every single day, and I'm not talking about other sporting events. Sure, there is great enthusiasm for events like the Olympics, but there, the focus is on the winners and how each person's country is doing.

In a regular marathon, there are winners, but most the people cheering don't care what place people finish in or what their time is. They're cheering for a human, not an outcome. And wouldn't the world be a better place if we had that same mentality every day, cheering for strangers to succeed for nothing more than the overall progress of humanity?

That was one of the things I loved most about New York City: it has a population so diverse that the only race is human (and the Marathon). Yes, it can be a very tough city to live in. The rent is high, the apartments are small, and the streets smell like trash in the summer. There are 8 million people and 2 million rats.[74] But it's for these reasons that New York also has a certain *"Jenny says qua,"* a certain energy or vibe to the city.

People live there for a reason; no one does it casually. The city is too hard for that. If you're there, you're passionate about something. And chances are NYC is #1 or #2 in that something. It's #1 in finance, theater, dance, stand-up, and pizza. It's arguably #1 but definitely #2 in fashion (Milan) and hot dogs (I'm partial to Skyline in Ohio). It's #2 in start-ups (San Francisco), entertainment (LA), improv (Chicago), law (DC), and Jay-Z songs ("Renegade").

While that brings an incredible energy to the city and means you can meet some of the most fascinating people in the world, it also means that people are focused on their life, not yours. It's why Keanu Reeves can ride the subway, and no one will bother him.

Some people take that focus as rudeness. New Yorkers aren't rude; they just aren't overly polite like those in the Midwest. And the absence of politeness isn't rudeness because true New Yorkers will help you when you're in need, and they'll cheer you on when you run 26.2 for no apparent reason.

But during my personal marathon of seeing all fifty states, I realized this isn't unique to New York. It took me leaving my favorite place to truly appreciate the diversity of the entire country. To get to know and understand people not just from Manhattan (New York) but Manhattan (Kansas); to see life in a city not of 8 million but 1,000, and to eat donuts not from a place nearby but a bakery in Fargo.

Because as I traveled, I came across people from all walks (or perhaps runs?) of life, who couldn't have been more different than me. There was Roland in Virginia, Shakespear in Florida, Bill in Iowa, and neck tattoo lady in South Dakota. And yet we were all able to relate, either through conversation, performance, or just being human. There was no competition, just connection. And everyone I met was running their own marathon, so why shouldn't I cheer them on?

"He's getting close," said one of my friends, tracking Vinnie's progress on an app. Adam, the tallest of our group, spotted him first and yelled out. We all started cheering for him as he came into view. He smiled and pumped his fist as he continued.

We stayed a short while longer to support more people coming by, people we had never met and probably never would. But we cheered anyway, as did all of the other millions of people watching. Then we headed into Central Park so we could find another spot along the route to do it all again.

---

74 I mean literal rats, not people who are wretched and scoundrelly.

#1 for Each State

Each state is number one in something, here's what it is:[75]

Alabama: Highest church attendance

Alaska: Most pilots

Arizona: Sunniest

Arkansas: Most dog owners

California: Safest for workers

Colorado: Lowest obesity

Connecticut: Most twin births

Delaware: Most moderates

Florida: Most identity thefts

Georgia: Busiest airport

Hawaii: Highest life expectancy

Idaho: Cheapest groceries

Illinois: Most average

Indiana: Most licensed drivers

Iowa: Lowest divorce rate

Kansas: Most claims to Superman

Kentucky: Best armed

Louisiana: Most residents born in state

Maine: Lowest violent crime

Maryland: Fewest accidental deaths

Massachusetts: Most college grads

Michigan: Most lighthouses

Minnesota: Best heart health

Mississippi: Most sleep per night

Missouri: Highest bankruptcy

Montana: Longest cat lifespans

Nebraska: Most homes with plumbing

Nevada: Most crime

New Hampshire: Lowest poverty rate

New Jersey: Most annoying to drive in

New Mexico: Most like Mexico in name

New York: Best in pizza and bagels

North Carolina Lowest teacher salary

North Dakota Lowest unemployment

Ohio: Highest library usage

Oklahoma: Most female criminals

Oregon: Most craft breweries

Pennsylvania: Craziest fans

Rhode Island: Lowest energy use

South Carolina: Most mobile homes

South Dakota: Best for retirement

Tennessee: Highest immunization

Texas: Most wind energy

Utah: Highest well-being

Vermont: Healthiest

Virginia: Most vanity plates

Washington: Friendliest for bicycles

West Virginia: Most heart attacks

Wisconsin: Biggest cheese producer

Wyoming: Cleanest air

SOURCES:
What Every State in America Is Best At by Frank Jacobs. Bigthink.com, November 2015.
What Every US State is Best At by Kate Peregrina. Thrillist.com, March 2015.
My own experiences.

---

75 Most results are per capita.

41. WISCONSIN

Put Up in Wisconsin
Milwaukee, WI. November 13, 2015

I finished zipping the zipper and snuggled into my sleeping bag. I wasn't camping in a tent or at an eighth-grade sleepover. No, I was in a cocoon blanket in the upstairs office of the CSz Milwaukee building in Milwaukee, Wisconsin.

After the marathon in New York, I had gone to California, Nevada, and then was headed to Illinois, where I would be doing a few stand-up shows. But first, I rode the train up to Milwaukee to play in a couple of ComedyS-portz matches and complete my forty-first state.

I had arrived in Milwaukee with just enough time to meet up with a fellow CSz member, Jacob, and go to Vanguard, a local bar known for their delicious sausages and love of pro wrestling. After our afternoon snack, we hung out at the CSz offices until the shows that night.

Milwaukee was where ComedySportz originally started in 1984, and the shows were always a blast; that night was no exception. After two great match-es, I hung out with more CSz members at the theater and was now attempting to go to sleep for the evening.

I originally planned to stay the night at the home of the founder of ComedySportz, Dick Chudnow, but he lived twenty-plus miles away from the office in the opposite direction of any of the players. He was an early sleeper and left the venue before the second show, so my only option at one o'clock in the morning was to take a $30 Uber ride to his place or sleep at CSz.

While it certainly would have been nice to have an actual bed in a house, I wasn't sure I could manage having a potentially long conversation with an Uber driver. Plus there was something compelling about sleeping on the couch in an office, a one-night foray into what it must have been like for that guy who lived at AOL for six months. And there was no way it could be worse than sleeping in a car.

So, against my bedder judgment,[76] I elected to try the office.

The space was nice. The couch was in the corner of a wide-open area where cubicles once sat. Now it was a makeshift room for improv classes and rounds of *Mafia/Werewolf*.[77] Offices lined the outside of the room and were rented out to another company. Each office had its own corporate-appropriate attempt at personalization. They also all had items that made you take a second, worried glance when you saw just their shadow at night: a tall lamp with a weird lampshade, cardboard cutouts of old advertisements, a plant that had grown into the silhouette of Freddy Krueger.

I wasn't scared to be sleeping alone in a multistory building with lots of weird rooms and who knows what kind of history, but I was on heightened alert. I remembered my conversation with Dick from earlier, when he told me sleeping at the office was an option.

"And if you don't want to take a cab or whatever that car thing is, you can always stay in the office," Dick offered.

"I wouldn't mind staying here," I said. "It could be fun."

"It's not bad at all. Most of the players have done it at some point," Dick replied.

"Anything I should know?" I asked.

"No." Dick paused. "Well, you should know about Roger."

"Roger?"

"Yeah, Roger. He likes to roam the building at night."

"What? Is Roger some type of ghost or something?" I joked.

"Yup."

I laughed. Dick didn't.

"Yeah, I can't believe I almost forgot to tell you about Roger," he continued. "Roger will hang out downstairs mostly. He doesn't go upstairs unless something is really wrong. Also, he's pretty harmless, though he does have a somewhat perverted sense of humor. And he's always making jokes that aren't

---

76 Get it? Because it's related to sleep?

77 The social games, not an incredibly awesome idea for a monster/mobster hybrid called were-mobsters.

funny."

I smiled and nodded. With any other person, I would have known they were joking, but Dick has an incredible sincerity about him even when he's saying or doing the most ridiculous things. He once passed around a roll of toilet paper to our large group at a fancy dinner, telling us to "take as much as you need." When I asked what we needed it for, he said, "You never know." I still have no idea what it was for, but I still have those two squares of TP.

"Okay, thanks for the heads up," I said, unsure of what to think.

I don't really believe in ghosts. An apparition of a dead person that becomes manifest to the living? I just can't see it. But if ghosts exist, I don't get why we assume they're nefarious. For every murderous tooth fairy ghost, there is a Casper the friendly ghost. Sure, there are the terrifying spirits from *Paranormal Activity* and *Ringu*, but there are also ghosts that played baseball in Iowa, made clay pots with former loved ones, and wrote secret messages to help young detectives solve neighborhood mysteries.[78]

And yet, none of that logic and reasoning stopped my mind from playing tricks on me while alone in the large, dark building. As the sole person (but possibly not the soul person) in the office, I became aware of every noise, every creak, every slight wind-against-the-window sound in the space.

I tried to drift off to sleep but couldn't. I felt unprepared for a potential ghost encounter. I was fairly certain ghosts weren't real, but that didn't mean I wanted to risk it. When I was afraid of possibly seeing a bear in Alaska, I created a plan, and it had helped calm my fears. So, I decided to create a plan for what I would do if I should wake up to see Roger hovering over me trying to draw inappropriate things on my face.

On the one hand, I knew who I was going to call if I did see a ghost. On the other was the watch I had forgotten to take off. The problem was that I wasn't sure if the Ghostbusters theme ever actually told you the number to their office. Maybe it was 867–5309; maybe Jenny was the receptionist.

I came up with a second plan in case Jenny wasn't affiliated with the parapsychologists. Some people claim ghosts appear when they have unfinished business in the world and they're stuck in limbo until they take care of it. I was skeptical. Think about all the things you've left unfinished in your life. There is no ghost of "One Day I'll Learn Guitar" or an apparition of "I'll Eventually Clean Out That Hallway Closet."

But if that were true, if ghosts were souls stuck here with unfinished business, and I was sleeping above a comedy club, maybe Roger's unfinished business was related to comedy. Maybe if he felt like he had a chance to perform, he would graduate out of the astral plane on Earth.

---

78 Shout out to my *Ghostwriter* fans.

So I started thinking of ghost puns. I figured if I did run into Roger, I could befriend him, and we could do a short sketch together. I thought through scenarios in my head until I came up with a killer scene idea.

Ghost A, played by me, would be a new ghost, someone who was afraid of public spooking and was in need of encouragement. Ghost B, played by Roger, would be the older, wiser ghost who shared his wisdom and got to say the punchlines.

Ghost A: I don't think I'm cut out to be a ghost. I can't scare anyone.
Ghost B: All you have to do is believe in yourself.
Ghost A: But I'm nervous; I've never spooked anyone before.
Ghost B: It's okay, just act supernatural.
Ghost A: You're right. Maybe I can do this.
Ghost B: That's the spirit.

And scene. It was perfect.

As I started to nod off, I smiled. I was safe. I would give Roger the closure he needed, and he wouldn't murder me. And even if he wasn't a fan of wordplay and didn't like the jokes I had written, he could do what most people do and just boo them.

42. DELAWARE

A Pooky Drive in Delaware
Yorklyn, DE. November 19, 2015

My hands gripped the steering wheel tighter, my knuckles turning white from tension. I was so nervous I didn't care that my hands were at "10 and 2" instead of the updated recommendation for "9 and 3." My Ford Fiesta rental car hugged the turns as rain fell outside. My heart beat faster than the fastest speed of the windshield wipers sloshing back and forth.

I was six days and 800 miles away from my ghost night in Milwaukee, but the experience still loomed in the back of my mind. After Wisconsin and Illinois, I flew back to the Northeast for some shows, including completing state #42 by doing a performance in Yorklyn, a small town at the northern tip of Delaware. It had been a warm, jovial experience, but now I was in a race for my life.

After the show, I foolishly wanted to reward myself for completing another state, so I looked up dessert places on Foursquare as I had done so many times before. The app showed a restaurant called Charcoal Pit in Wilmington that claimed to have delicious milkshakes, so I set the GPS for sweetness.

What I didn't know was that Google Maps was going take me through what I assumed was called Serial Killer Forest. I cursed Google for not having an option for "No scary routes."

It was pitch dark as I drove through the woods on backcountry roads. There were no street lamps or reflectors in the middle, the only light coming from the moon, my headlights, and my phone, which showed my route and zero bars of service.

I had seen enough scary movies to know that this was how the horror began. A lone person driving by himself after a fun night, excited for the future, and without a care in the world. Except I had a care in the world, I had one for every shadowy figure I saw in the dark.

The rain fell harder as a fog started to creep in. I thought about turning my brights back on, but I had turned them off because, although it was harder to see the road, it meant I was less likely to see the chainsaw wielding skin-wearers in overalls that were inevitably standing by the side of it.

I thought back to a story my mom liked to tell about me as a kid. Once, while we drove through a wooded area at night, kid Drew proclaimed aloud, "These woods are pooky." Not "spooky," but "pooky" because I was five years old and adorable. As an adult, the woods were still pooky, and the more I drove, the pookier the forest seemed to grow.

My mistrust of the dark came from my brothers, who psychologically tormented me because I was the baby of the family.

David, my middle brother and the one who traveled the Midwest with me, used to make me watch scary movies with him when I was far too young and impressionable. I remember watching *Children of the Corn* and *It* as a child, and now I don't like cornfields or clowns. I'm convinced that the most terrifying thing possible is the image of a clown emerging from a cornfield.

Worse than that was my oldest brother, Adam, who liked to "prank" me—that is if scaring an innocent child can be considered a "prank." When I was in the first grade, every day when I came home from school, I would go into my room and put my backpack in my closet like a good student. But one day that changed.

I went to put my bag in the closet like I had done every day before, but as I started to set it down, I saw a single eye staring at me from inside the dark recesses of the wardrobe. I threw my bag in the air and ran screaming down the hallway. Adam had been waiting for me so he could jump out when I opened the door; turns out he didn't even have to move, I saw his eyeball, and that was enough. That was the last day I ever put my backpack away.

I was about to reenact that screaming in Delaware when the woods started to clear. I began to relax but soon realized it wasn't a good kind of clearing. As the moonlight shined through the opening of trees, I noticed four or five different "No Trespassing" signs posted on both sides of the road. I couldn't tell in the darkness, but I had to assume that the signs were hanging there not by nails from Home Depot but from bones of unsuspecting comedians who were looking for milkshakes.

I audibly gulped, pushed the Fiesta past fifty miles an hour on the thirty-five mph road, and reentered the forest, the clearing shrinking away in the rearview mirror.

Just as I thought it couldn't get any worse, I saw headlights coming from the opposite direction. I mentally pendulummed back and forth about whether the car meant I was nearing civilization or whether that urban legend where people flash their lights at the people they're going to kill was about to come true.

The car passed, and I didn't dare look at the driver. I didn't want to see what, if anything, was sharing that back road with me. As I started losing my grip on reality, I started to come to grips with accepting that this was how it was all going to end: death by a Delaware killer.

In a way, it seemed fitting. The things we love most can so often be the death of us; for me, it would all be because of a milkshake. I consoled myself by saying at least I was doing something I loved. So many people pass away without achieving their dreams, but if a *Silence of the Lambs* wannabe killer murdered me for my skin that night, I could at least take solace in the fact that I didn't have any major regrets. I wouldn't complete my goal of all fifty states, but at least I was trying.

Suddenly, up ahead, I saw a reflective yellow sign. As I turned a bend, I saw that it marked an upcoming street. Shortly after, the woods started to dissipate, and I came upon a more industrialized intersection. I turned right and zoomed down a standard suburban street and hit a highway. My knuckles stayed clenched the entire drive until I finally made it to Charcoal Pit.

The cell signal returned to my phone. The rained softened to a drizzle, and the people around seemed to be normal, not human-skin-wearing psychopaths. Maybe part of my nomad journey was about facing my fears, of heading into the darkness and coming out a little wiser on the other side. Or maybe I was overblowing a simple drive through some woods. It was impossible to know how close I had come to death that night, but at least I knew I was living without regrets.

I stepped out of the car and into the Pit. I don't know if it was the adrenaline or just the recipe of the restaurant, but it was a darn good milkshake.

Times I Thought I Might Die

Rational or not, I worked myself into a bit of panic during my drive in Delaware. Truth be told, it wasn't the first time I had the thought, "This is how I die." Here are some of the obituaries that would have been written had I passed when I thought I might.

Yorklyn, DE. A young spoken word artist was killed last week while driving through Serial Killer Forest outside of Yorklyn. Locals were surprised anyone would drive such a dangerous road at night but were not surprised by the results. What remains, mostly just teeth and a weird nub he had on his shoulder, will be sent to his family.

Boulder City, CO. The body of a frail, feeble man-child was found by hikers on the Rocky Mountain Trail yesterday. After much investigation, it was concluded that the man was visiting Pikes Peak when the sight of the sun caused him to sneeze. The power of the sneeze sent his body over the edge, and a large gust of wind carried his dainty frame two hundred miles north onto the Timber Lake Trail. Justin Timberlake, who has no connection to the trail or deceased man-child, could not be reached for comment.

Stuart, IA. The remains of a "comedian" were found in a farmhouse near Stuart earlier today. The "comedian" was on a road trip to visit all fifty states and thought the home was hosting an open mic. The "comedian" entered the home, started telling puns, and was shot on sight. Police are not charging the homeowner, ruling the death as a clear case of self-defense.

Juneau, AK. A gullible man died at the Mendenhall Glacier Trail a few days ago when he fell for the "just sing to a bear to make him go away" prank popular with rangers. His last words were reportedly, "It's Friday, Friday, gotta get down on Friday." The mauling happened on a Sunday.

Sunshine, LA. A farmer is reporting that he found the stickly figure of a pasty white man dead on his farm this afternoon. The farmer noticed his cows were all gathered around in a menacing circle and went to investigate. He found the body of an aging comedian in the middle of the herd as various bovine chewed his body like cud. It is unclear how this will affect the taste of the cows' milk.

43. MISSOURI

I Love You
St. Louis, MO. December 20, 2015

Rachel got up to throw our trash away, and as soon as she left the table, I turned to Felicia.

"Alright, so now that she's gone, is there anything I should know about her?" I joked.

The three of us were at Donut Drive-In in St. Louis, Missouri, and Rachel's and my relationship had just passed a few big milestones.

The first milestone was that we had just survived a fifteen-hour car ride together. After Delaware, I returned for a quick stay in New York before heading to Ohio for Thanksgiving. From there, David and I drove to Texas where I was leading a couple of humor programs and guest teaching his classes at Texas A&M. Then it was back to New York to do some stand-up and to meet up with Rachel.

She was heading to California at the start of the new year for her last clinical before earning her doctor in physical therapy from Columbia University. During her time out West, she was keeping her stuff in her old bedroom at her parents' place in St. Louis. So, we packed up her things in an SUV rental and drove the 1,000 miles from NYC to STL.

And, after fifteen hours in 116 cubic feet of space together, we didn't hate each other. In fact, we still very much liked each other. During our drive, we chatted, answered questions, played car games, and listened to music, rocking out to T. Swift and Yeezy.[79]

The second, bigger milestone was that we had met each other's parents. First, we stopped in Cincinnati on the way to St. Louis and had dinner with my mom and brothers. We ate at a grilled cheese cafe, I introduced her to Graeter's ice cream, and we stayed the night at my mom's place. Then we continued on to her hometown where I met her parents, brother, and sister-in-law. We had dinner at an Italian restaurant, went to see the brewery lights at Anheuser-Busch, and stayed the night at her parent's place. It was like we were back in high school, and the only thing left was for our moms to get into a fight at a PTA bake sale.

Both meetings had gone well. My family loved her—how could they not?—though Adam was rightfully hesitant of her fanship of the St. Louis Cardinals. And her family seemed to like me. Her brother and I connected over our mutual love of technology, her mom and I connected over the necessity of baked goods, and her dad and I connected over his great dad jokes.

But the third, biggest, and scariest milestone was meeting one of her best friends, Felicia.

I wasn't nervous for her to meet my family because she's awesome, and so are they. And I wasn't that nervous to meet hers because parents typically love me—they find out I'm a momma's boy, learn that I don't really drink, and see that I'm about as threatening as a Goomba on the first level of Super Mario.

But meeting someone's best friend? That's different. Their expectations are different, their perspective is different, and their influence is different. A parent is an external factor giving input; a best friend is an extension of themselves, and "if the best friend don't like you, the girl don't like you."[80]

Luckily, it seemed to be going well with Felicia. She was impressed with my decision to be a nomad and surprised I was actually kinda funny for an engineer. We also connected over our college days, the joys of being from the Midwest, and of course, delicious donuts.

We had agreed to meet at Donut Drive-In because it was central for both Felicia and us, and it happened to be the best donut shop in the United States (according to Rachel's expert and experienced opinion). The "Best Donut Shop on Route 66" (according to the papers on the wall in the shop) didn't do super fancy donuts, but they did the basics spectacularly well, including a Cinnamon Twist that is Rachel's most favoritest of all donuts.[81]

It was there, when Rachel got up to throw away some trash, that I asked

---

79 Regardless of their actual feelings for each other, Kanye and Taylor work well together on my iPod.

80 This isn't actually attributed to anyone that I know of, I just thought it sounded more authoritative in quotes.

81 I'll admit, it's pretty good but not quite a S'mores Long John.

my question to get the inside scoop on what I should know about the Hobbes to my Calvin.

Felicia thought for a moment. "Has she told you the 'I love you' story yet?"

"Oooh, she has an 'I love you' story?" I asked. "She hasn't said anything about it. What happened?"

"Oh, this is going to be fun," Felicia replied, a smirk on her face.

Rachel returned and saw us both smiling. "Uh oh, what did you say, Felicia?"

"What? Me? Nothing. I just mentioned Noah's name."

Rachel's face dropped. "I was gone for two seconds! How could that have possibly come up?"

Felicia and I smiled. "So, what happened with Noah?" I asked.

After some hesitancy and playful prodding, Rachel finally relented.

"Noah was a friend of mine in college, and that's all we were, friends. Well, apparently he started liking me, and I never realized it, until one day we were chatting and, out of nowhere, he says 'I love you.' And I was surprised, and I didn't know what to say. So . . ."

Rachel stopped. I waited for her to continue but it didn't seem like she was going to on her own.

"So . . . What did you say?" I asked.

"So . . . I didn't say anything," Rachel continued, pausing another moment. "I just gave him a slow, awkward, thumbs up and walked away."

I laughed out loud.[82]

"A thumbs up?" I confirmed. Felicia nodded.

"Thank you for laughing at my ridiculousness," Rachel pouted.

"What? You have to admit that is funny. A friend confessed his love to you, and you gave the nonverbal equivalent of 'cool.'"

"I know," Rachel conceded, "it was just really embarrassing. And thank you, Felicia; you were supposed to be on my side."

"What? He asked if there was anything he should know about you. I thought that was appropriate."

"It was definitely appropriate," I confirmed. I got up and gave Rachel a hug. "It's cute, although I'm not sure how to feel since I didn't get a thumbs up the first time I said it to you . . ."

"That's because I said it back!" Rachel defended.

"I know; I'm glad you did," I replied with a smile. "I'm also glad we both have embarrassing 'I love you' stories."

---

82 A for real laugh out loud, not the lies we tell people when we type lol at something that is moderately whimsical.

It was true. In fact, I had two. The first time someone I was dating said, "I love you," my response was, "Thank you." That's the wrong answer. The correct response, the only one someone is really looking for, is "I love you, too."

I thought I'd figured that out, so when my next girlfriend said, "Drew, I want you to know, I love you," I responded, "I love you, as well." She smiled and then asked, "How much?" And I was like "whaaaaaa?" Because I didn't know there would be follow-up questions. So I responded, "I love you very much." And she said, "No, like how much do you love me?"

And as an engineer, you can't ask me something like that because then I'll try to give you an accurate answer. So I thought about it and said, "I love you eight much. Eight love units, that's what I feel."

Because I don't know how to quantify something like that. Do you use a number system? Do you use a metaphor, like "I love you as much as the moon loves the stars?" What does that even mean? That I don't actually love you at all because they are inanimate objects with no capacity for emotion? Or do you compare it to something else, like "I love you more than *House of Cards* but less than *Game of Thrones*?"

I proceeded to tell Felicia these examples of my own awkwardness with the phrase, and she gave her approval of the relationship, "I guess you two awkward nerds are perfect for each other."

It was the kindest thing she could have said.

We chatted a while longer before I had to get back on the road for Ohio. We said the standard "nice to finally meet yous," gave the usual hugs, and parted ways.

As I sat in the car to head back to Rachel's place, I commented, "I thought that went well; she's great."

Rachel rolled her eyes. "Yeah, you two really bonded there at the end."

"That's a good thing! I want her to like me because, as you may remember, I love you." I said.

She put out her hand, stuck out her thumb, and turned it down. I feigned a gasp.

"Fine," she replied, "I love you, too."

44. UTAH

The Place on the Plate
Arches National Park. December 30, 2015

I was taking a break from emails when I saw the sign that opened up my eyes to the wonders of Moab, Utah.

Rachel and I were driving from Missouri to California so that she could start her last clinical in Palo Alto. In the ten days since we had finished our fifteen-hour car trip together, I had returned to Ohio for Christmas and then flew back to St. Louis in time for Rachel and me to start a new thirty-hour drive to the Bay Area.

Originally, we planned to drive the southern route across Texas, particularly since it was winter, but El Niño had made that route the more treacherous journey. Instead, we went north through Colorado, and now Utah, where we passed the sign.

I didn't know the place by name but instantly recognized the iconic image; it was the red arch rock that was on nearly every single Utah license plate I had ever seen, including the car driving directly in front us.

"That's the place on the license plate," I said pointing to the billboard.

"Huh?" Rachel asked, not having been privy to the thoughts in my head.

"That place, Moab, is what's on all the Utah plates we've seen," I clarified.

"Oh, the Arches National Park?" she responded. She knew a lot more about cool parks than me.

"Yeah, it's an exit off this highway. I wonder if we could visit it."

I brought up my phone and did a little research. The city of Moab was a thirty-minute drive off of I-70. From there, the licensed-plated Delicate Arch was an additional forty-five-minute drive into the Arches National Park. The hike from there was another forty-five minutes to reach the landmark.

I doubled the numbers. "If we wanted to see that rock hole, it would add about four hours to the trip, though an hour and a half of that would be hiking."

"So, two and a half hours of added driving?" Rachel calculated.

"Yeah, but some of that is in the park area, so it's probably pretty cool looking. We could drive to Moab tonight, find a hotel, and then go hiking in the morning before getting back on the road."

Rachel thought for a moment before asking, "What's the temperature supposed to be like tomorrow?"

Oh right, it was December in Utah, and we hadn't really packed for winter hiking. "Looks like it's a high of twenty-five degrees. Light flurries possible."

And thus the deliberation began. We had a bit of a schedule to keep to get Rachel moved in at her new spot. We also already had thirty-plus hours of driving over the course of five days that we didn't necessarily want to add to. I wasn't a fan of having to backtrack, and we didn't have the right gear to do it well.

But we both loved adventure, and one thing I was starting to learn from my year as a nomad was that sometimes backtracking was okay, or even necessary, to truly enjoy the journey. Sure, it was out of the way, but it would be fun. We weren't attempting to set a record for fastest time from St. Louis to Palo Alto, and we got no reward for "powering straight through." Our only real constraints were the ones we gave ourselves. Plus, we'd get to say we'd been to the place on the plate.

After some additional discussion and planning, we decided to do it. We made our way to Moab, found dinner and a hotel, prepped for the next day, and went to sleep.

The next morning, the alarm "rehn rehn rehned" earlier than I would have liked, but we had to get an early start, so we weren't too delayed. We showered, grabbed some calories from the continental breakfast, and made our way outside. The "light flurries" overnight had dropped two inches of snow on the ground.

"Do you think the snow will be a problem?" Rachel asked.

"Nah," I said, hopeful, and not willing to suggest we had gone out of our way for nothing.

We cleared the snow off Rachel's car, hopped in, and headed to the park.

The drive through Arches National Park was beautiful. A light dusting of snow covered the red rock, making the landscape look like an assortment of frosted ginger snap cookies. The main streets had been plowed but the smaller roads to get to the arches were covered in snow and ice. We had a few close calls with the ditches to the side but made it to the Delicate Arches path relatively unscathed.

Weather.com measured the temperature at a brisk twenty-three degrees. Rachel and I bundled in layers, combinations of long underwear, workout pants, long sleeved shirts, and jackets. I made the hike in gym shoes with double socks, and Rachel did it in yellow rain boots seemingly from the cover of *Singing in the Rain*.[83]

The hike to the top was gorgeous. The sun warmed the park in a cloudless sky, the snow slowly melting with each step we took. There were incredible views of the sandstone towers and sections of precarious walkways along ridges dropping into the landscape.

As we ascended, my personal temperature went from "It's pretty chilly out here" to "It's not so bad" to "Man, it's kind of hot." After nearly forty-five minutes of hiking, we made our way around a bend and reached the summit.

We both stopped as we caught our breath, each exhale visible in the cold. Beyond the mist of our CO_2 was the Delicate Arch. It was just like in the picture on the license plate, but prettier, more majestic, and without numbers like CRC-4103 obstructing the view.

We took a seat and ate a snack from our bag, quenching our thirst with stupid lemoned water we had gotten at the hotel. A few months ago, I would have never thought to stop for this side quest. I would have seen the sign and thought, "hmmph" and that's it. But after experiences like Maine and near-misses like Kansas, I realized it wasn't backtracking if the detour had a purpose.

And I was happy to be sharing the experience with someone I cared about. This whole cross-country trip was a lot more fun because Rachel was with me.

Don't get me wrong; I liked roadtripping on my own. I did some of my best thinking while driving by myself out on the open road. It was just me, my music, and my brain. And until self-driving cars become a thing we all freak out about and then grow to love, being behind the wheel is one of the few times in modern society where you are forced to be away from your devices and encouraged to be with your own thoughts. It's like taking a shower: you're in your own bubble, you have to be conscious but not hyperaware, and

---

83 But not actually from the cover as they wore bright yellow raincoats on the movie poster but regular dress shoes and heels, which seemed like terrible attire for sloshing around in water.

you're naked.[84]

As a result, my solo drives often served as a time to think through some of my programs or work on stand-up material, using Google's Voice-to-Text technology to record my thoughts into Evernote. I usually had to clean up the recordings later (no Google, I said "adrenaline," not "the Ritalin"), but it was helpful to get the ideas out of my head and into a more reliable storage system.

But that drive and hike were more fun because Rachel was there. We talked, shared music, and played car games like Bust-a-Rhyme, Mind Meld, and the classic License Plate Game. And now we were at the place on the plate.

After a brief break, we took pictures and made our way across a field of ice to take a selfie under the arch. We stayed a while longer before heading back down the trail, to the car, and on the road.

The detour had cost us an additional four and a half hours in time, and we had to backtrack for roughly half of it. It wasn't efficient, but it was fun, and the experience paid it all back tenfold in the form of a happy memory and a sick selfie.[85]

---

84 That's just a joke; I've never driven fully naked. I feel weird driving with no shirt on.
85 To see the Delicate Arch selfie, visit tarv.in/utah

Funny Google Translations

Google's Voice-to-Text technology is incredibly helpful for taking notes in the car. However, it's not always perfect. Here are some of the notes I've recorded while driving and what they were supposed to say.

WHAT I SAID	WHAT GOOGLE TRANSLATED
I went to Texas A&M.	I went to Texas Animal.
I packed two ties and dress shoes.	I packed popeyes and rescues.
Check in with Phill Nosworthy.	Check in with still not working.
Write down travel rules.	Write down scrabble rules.
Are you using?	Hairy uses.
The applause died down.	The lies died down.
I was nervous for the performance.	I was nervous for the Mormons.
I lived nomadically.	I lived pneumatically.
I didn't grow up the wealthiest.	I didn't grope the wealthiest.
I wanted to give him mad props.	I wanted to give him math problems.
I've been Andrew Tarvin.	I've been out of carbon.
Google, you're an idiot.	Google, I'm an idiot.

45. NEVADA

Happy New Year
Las Vegas, NV. December 31, 2015

We stood at the floor-to-ceiling windows looking out at the Vegas strip. The lights of the casinos lit up the midnight sky off to our right. The desert lurked in the darkness, hidden to the left.

We were at the Palms Place Hotel in Las Vegas, Nevada, a half-fortuitous/half-planned stop on our drive out West. Our room looked as if it had been plucked straight from the set of a Bond film. The bed was low, the ceilings were high, and everything was pristine and modern. It was a far fancier place than I should have been in, but HotelTonight had pulled through last minute for quite a place to stay.

The view was beautiful but paled in comparison to the beauty that was standing next to me. Rachel stood by my side in an elegant blue dress heightened by her black heels. Her brown-auburn hair fell in loose curls to her shoulders as her smile shined brighter than any of the lights outside. I wore my blue suit, the one that made it kind of look like I had a butt, in an attempt to be worthy of her beauty, and we sipped gin and tonics.

The TV behind us was on, the crowd shouting out the numbers as we inched our way closer to midnight. Half of the world had already entered the New Year, and those of us in Pacific Time were about to join them. A short while before, I had talked to my mom and brothers who were now in the future of 2016; they assured me things were going well so far.

I felt as if I was in a movie, or perhaps an award-winning, long-running

TV series. It wasn't the beginning or middle of the story arc but the end. I had been living for nine months as a nomad and had overcome challenges big and small, adjusting to a life of constant travel and living out of two bags. And this was the last scene of Andrew Tarvin 2015. I was headed toward happily ever after, at least until the next season began, and the nomad storyline served as a cliffhanger during the break.

I looked out at the lit-up windows of the hotels along the strip, realizing each one had their own characters living their own stories. For many of the people standing out there under their own lights, 2015 had been a year of joy: people had gotten promoted or moved to a new home or had finally become a series regular after years of background work. For others, it was one of heartbreak or strife or moderate annoyance. Some would be sad to see it go; others would be happy for the arbitrary restart. Many would continue to write 2015 on things for months to come.

Soon, the story of 2016 would begin as 2015 became a recent memory. As time marched forward, certain memories of the past year would fade away. I would forget about the minor stresses, the inconveniences, and the thousands of tiny things I had let affect me throughout the year that no longer mattered.

But I wouldn't forget the experiences, I wouldn't lose the lessons I learned, and I would hold on to the moments that mattered as they played in my head like a "Previously On" montage to the next episodes of my life.

I had no idea what the new year had in store for me: my completion of all fifty states, my move back to New York, or my writing of this very moment in a cafe in Brooklyn. But at that moment, I wasn't worried about what was to come, or what had been. I was just enjoying what was.

And that was one of the lessons I had learned over the previous nine months: to appreciate the present moment.

New Year's has always been an exciting time for me because it's when I check in to see how I did on my goals from the previous year, and I start thinking about what I'll accomplish next. And I know you don't need an arbitrary day to reflect on what you've accomplished, just as you don't need one to remember to say thanks, to tell your significant other how much you love them, or to plant a tree, but it was a good excuse. And there is tremendous value in reviewing and planning your time, but if you reflected too much on the past or focused too much on the future, you could easily miss the now.

I turned my attention to Rachel and took a sip of my gin and tonic. It was crafted by mine truly and was one of the many things she was phenomenal at making, along with cookies and me happy. It was my favorite alcoholic drink thanks to a trip to Madrid two years ago. I didn't often drink, but it was a nice way to cap off the year (especially since we couldn't find a milkshake at that hour).

I took the time to appreciate the beauty of the situation: the setting, the scenery, the company, the relationship, the drink, and the moment. I didn't need to be at an overpriced bar where they served free champagne and terrible hors d'oeuvres, and I certainly didn't want to be standing in a throng of people, freezing, just to see a mechanical ball drop. I was happy exactly where I was.

The crowd on TV reached the end of their chant. "Three! Two! One!"

Rachel smiled. I smiled. Right now, everything was perfect.

"Happy New Year!"

CALIFORNIA

County Road 20909
Somewhere in CA on the way to LA. January 1, 2016

We cruised south on I-15 as we headed toward California. Rachel was behind the wheel, and I was in the passenger seat. It was the first day of the New Year, and our fourth day driving west. Things had gone relatively smoothly thus far, but things were about to change.

As we crossed from Nevada into California, Rachel and I casually chatted and starting thinking about our plans for the upcoming months. There were a lot of cars on the road, likely fellow "New Year's Eve in Vegas" partygoers, but traffic was moving smoothly. Car after car whizzed past us on the left, including, at one point, a low-riding Enzo Ferrari that looked like it was straight from *The Fast and The Furious* set.

But twenty miles after crossing the California border, we saw brake lights up ahead. As we approached the stopped cars, all we could see in front of us was traffic. We had been using an old school on-the-dash Magellan GPS for much of our drive, saving our phones for more important tasks like texting,[86] but any time there was traffic, it was Google Maps to the rescue.

I pulled up the app on Rachel's phone and put in our destination.

"There is a forty-five-minute slow-down ahead. You can save . . . Yadda yadda yadda."

Of course, we'll take the detour; that's why we were using the app. We

---

86 But not the person who was driving. Stay safe, kids.

pulled off at the exit, as instructed by the nice voice, and got behind a line of cars all doing the same. A few cars ahead of us was the aforementioned Ferrari with its sexy tail lights and low-riding frame.

We made a right and then a near immediate left onto a road that Google called County Road 20909. The Magellan didn't call the road anything because it didn't know it existed. And understandably so because this was not a major street, nor a minor street, or really a street at all. It was a dirt road.

We were hesitant to take the detour, but there were loads of cars in front of us and plenty more behind us. The road was pretty hard, and it looked like we could save at least an hour of sitting in traffic, so we made our way.

As we drove, Rachel and I enjoyed the scenery of dirt and cacti (cactus? cactuses?) on either side of us. The sun hung about three-quarters of the way in the sky, a few more hours of daylight left, as the dust kicked off the tires behind us. Off in the distance we could see that the traffic on the highway was still completely stopped and that, however unlikely, this detour was working. For now.

The first sign of trouble was that the road started developing bigger and bigger dirt holes. Ahead of us, one of those square-looking Scions didn't see a car-sized ditch and got stuck in one of the gaps in the road. Didn't the driver know you can't fit a square car into a round pothole? Strangers were already helping the lunchbox-on-wheels, so we carefully navigated around.

I caught a glimpse of the Ferrari ahead of us, nearly eclipsed by the dust kicking up around it. Rachel and I were both surprised anyone in such a nice car would see the dirt road and think, "Yeah, this is definitely the best route for my $200,000 hunk of sexy metal."

The second sign of trouble came a few miles later as the entire caravan of cars came to a complete stop. We waited a few minutes in the car before deciding to step out, as just about everyone else had.

"Anyone know what's going on?" someone from the car in front of us shouted.

"Nope. There's a bunch of cars stopped ahead," someone else shared in one of those obvious statements you make in general small talk.

We chatted casually for a few minutes and quickly determined that 100 percent of the people were there because of Google Maps. We joked about how this wasn't ideal but would be a funny story to tell our friends, everyone more or less calm about the inconvenient situation. A few people threw on some music and people continued to talk. I wondered if we were in some type of Pepsi commercial.

I decided to find out what was going on and left Rachel with the car.

I took off in a light jog toward the front of the queue, passing the Ferrari and its riders as I went. With every step I took, and every move I made, I thought of Biggie Smalls—and noticed that the road was turning more and more into sand. About a mile up, I found the source of the backup: a Toyota Camry stuck in the sandy road, its tires spinning with no traction.[87]

A small crowd had gathered with a few attempting to push the car free. I joined the group, and we tried everything we could to get the car to move. We placed sticks under the tires to try to give it more traction, we had them go forward and reverse multiple times, and we tried pushing down so that it might catch the road. Nothing seemed to work until probably thirty minutes later, when we finally found success rocking the car back and forth until it sprang free.

The car drove off into the setting sun for all of twenty feet before it got stuck again.

By this time, other cars were attempting their own detours. There was no way to turn back as it was a single road lined by sand, bushes, and cacti/cactus/cactuses. Some people veered off and just drove through the bush—I'm sure doing wonders for their grill and suspension. Others waited patiently, hoping they'd be able to get through. The sun continued to drop in the sky.

Those off on the side of the road came up with a theory as to what was happening. The cars were fine, if they didn't stop. But as soon as they did, the tires would sink into the sand, and they'd lose all traction. From there, they'd need to be rocked out of the hole.

Most of the group ran up to help the Camry again. I ran back toward Rachel, stopping along the way to tell people what was happening.

"The road turns to sand up there. It's okay if you keep going, but as soon as you stop, you get stuck. So, wait until the car in front of you has made it, and then go, without slowing down."

I felt like the announcer at the world's worst roller coaster ride.

I made it back to Rachel's car where she had gone from calm and collected to worried and stressed. I didn't realize I had been gone for close to an hour, and I hadn't picked up my phone because I was busy pushing and had no cell service. The sun was setting, and she wasn't sure what to do, where I was, or what was going on.

Her concerns were quite valid. It was starting to get dark and navigating the sandy road would be incredibly difficult, if not impossible, at night. There was nothing within walking distance of where we were and who knew how cold the desert would get at night or what type of Tremor worms might be nearby. I felt a bit panicked but remained calm on the outside, reassuring

---

[87] I wondered if it was the same dumb *Camry* as Massachusetts, delaying me yet again, but it seemed incredibly unlikely.

myself that at least there weren't a lot of pooky trees around.

I filled her in on what was happening and then headed back to the front of the queue to help cars as they got stuck. Each car took its time crossing the sanded part, many of them getting stuck at least once, each one taking away precious daylight. This was the danger of taking the road less traveled: there were more likely to be hazards.

Soon it was the Ferrari's turn. I assumed it would do well, breezing along as if it were on air. It did not. It got stuck as well, so we all gathered behind to help. As we were pushing the car along, the man next to me said, "I did not expect to be pushing a Ferrari in the sand today." I verbally agreed but then thought about how weird it would have been if he had expected that.

The Enzo sprang free, and I went back to meet Rachel. We discussed the merits of taking the detour while we waited for our turn at the sandy obstacle course. We had no way of knowing the road would turn into sand and Google Maps had already helped me more times than I could possibly count. Yes we were in a bit of a precarious situation, but considering all of the detours I had taken on my journey and the adventures they had led to, I was comfortable with trusting the voice in the phone.

I tried to ease the stress in the car and told Rachel about my "harrowing" drive in Delaware and how delicious the milkshake tasted after the whole ordeal. We laughed and decided that we'd stop at the first In N Out we found and reward ourselves with a Neapolitan shake; we'd go from desert to dessert.

As we approached the starting line of the "don't let the car drag" race, Rachel started to get more nervous. She decided she didn't want to do it, so I hopped in the driver's seat—the first time I had driven her car, a stick, the entire trip—and made it through with no problem.

Well, okay, one slight problem. I hit a particularly sandy spot and shifted at the wrong time, causing the car to sink into the sand. Luckily by this time there was a group of Samaritans just waiting to help each car that got stuck. They swooped in like a pit crew at a NASCAR race and got the car going again in seconds. They were so clutch.

I made it the rest of the way, and we got to the end of County Road 20909. We made a left and then a right and were finally back on the highway—three hours later. The sun had completely set, the stars had come out, and the traffic jam on I-15 had long been cleared.

47. WEST VIRGINIA

The Worst Show of the Tour
Charleston, WV. January 25, 2016

My watch crept past 22:45. It had already been a long day, and it was only getting longer.

I was at the "world famous" Empty Glass in Charleston, West Virginia, for the city's longest running open mic night. I had found the show at the last minute because my planned engagement, an event at West Virginia University, had been canceled due to winter storms that had completely thrown off my schedule.

I was nearing the completion of all fifty states, so after moving Rachel into her place in Palo Alto and staying there for a few weeks, I was back on the East Coast to take care of West Virginia, North Carolina, and Maryland. The plan was to fly to New York, rent a car, and do a 1,300 mile loop over the course of seven days. But thanks to a "crippling and historic" blizzard/Nor'easter/extratropical cyclone ice storm named Winter Storm Jonas aka Snowzilla, the closest I could get to New York was Atlanta.

After reaching ATL, I got snowed into Georgia for three days before renting a car and heading north to this music open mic, the only thing resembling a show I could find that would still allow me to check off West Virginia as a state.

A less anal-retentive person might have decided to reschedule a trip to the Mountain State, but I couldn't. I had to complete my checklist and I had less than forty days to do it. Plus, I was building up toward an epic finale in

Hawaii in February; there was no way I wanted to come back to West Virginia after that.

This drive to complete things was a blessing and a curse. It was great for things like finishing projects and accomplishing goals; it wasn't so great for binge-watching TV or eating an entire package of Double Stuf Oreos to "complete the task."

And so I waited.

The show that would bring me one step closer to my goal was supposed to start at 10:00 p.m., but the host band, Groove Heavy, had arrived thirty minutes late. They took their time in setting up their equipment, not in a rush for the five total people in the bar: me, two bartenders, and two friends of the bartenders.

I loaded the Reddit app on my phone for the eighteenth time since arriving and tried to find something to pass the time as the band did sound checks for the drums, bass, guitar, keyboard, microphone, and my patience.

Eventually, one the band members announced into the microphone, "If you're here for the open mic, you can sign up at the front of the stage."

I was the only one who moved to sign up.

The host continued, "We're going to take a ten-minute break and then get started."

I wasn't sure if you could call it a break if you hadn't started yet, but at least the show was happening soon. Since I was the only person to sign up, I took solace in the fact that I would at least be first and could hopefully get back to my hotel before midnight.

As I waited, I wondered when they were going to change the ambiance of the room to be more conducive to a show. As it stood at the moment, the room was brightly lit with fluorescents overhead and an added glow from TVs mounted on the walls. The bartenders and their friends hung out at the bar as I sat at one of the tables off to the side, toward the back. Together, with the stage, we created an equilateral triangle with fifteen-foot sides and an area of roughly 97.43 triangle feet, not exactly the best geometry for an intimate show.

Twenty minutes later, the band returned. The guitarist stepped up to the mic. "Alright, let's get started with the show. We're going to warm things up with a few songs of our own, and then after that, we're going to hear from Drew Tarbin."

Close enough. Both to my name and how I felt about the show. I was only a few minutes away from being able to check off the state and go to sleep.

I waited for the bar to go into show mode, possibly for more people to show up or for those who were there to move toward the front, the lights to drop, or at least the TVs to be turned off. None of those things happened.

The band started playing and, despite the fact that it was a Monday in Charleston, West Virginia, at 11:10 p.m. in a bar with TVs on, they were surprisingly great. Their sound was a mix of R&B and EDM that seemed to match the chill vibe of the situation.

Their first song seamlessly transitioned into their second. And then into their third. Then their fourth. Then, finally, after twenty-five minutes of non-stop playing, they ended on a huge crescendo resulting in light applause from the five of us watching.

"Thank you," the guitarist said. "Now for our first open mic'er, give it up for Drew Tarbin."

At least he was consistent.

I headed to the stage and started my set.

"Hello everyone, I'm Drew Tarvin, and I am on a tour to speak or perform in all fifty states. With this show tonight, it'll be my forty-seventh state."

Polite smiles came from the audience. It was the warmest reaction I'd get the entire set. It's not that they disliked what I said; they just didn't care, like New Yorkers on the subway when a group of kids start break-dancing.

I went into my dramatic reading of dumb jokes.

"A guy asked me if I wanted a free fish. So I asked, 'What's the catch?'"

Silence. Utter, absolute, painful silence. So I tried another.

"Hey, remember that time we ate those cute pistachios? Yeah, that was pretty nuts."

Nothing. I could hear them blinking at me. I could see the neurons firing inside their heads as they wondered why I was even there. I could feel the general disdain for my presence, and I knew I was bombing.

Bombing on stage is a painful experience and is amplified when doing stand-up comedy. If you're playing music and no one is paying attention, it doesn't really impact your performance. If you do spoken word and the audience doesn't react, it doesn't feel great, but you can still stay committed to your piece.

But stand-up comedy is a conversation, where the audience's contribution is laughter. And when there is no laughter, it's like asking someone a question and having them just stare at you, like what you said is either so stupid it doesn't warrant a response or they hate you so much that they don't care to acknowledge your existence at all.

Worst of all, I couldn't blame them for their harsh silence. They hadn't come to the bar to hear comedy that night; they came to hang out, talk to friends, and listen to music. It was my responsibility as a performer to match the situation of the room. The truth is it's never the fault of the audience if a set doesn't go well. It's not their job to laugh; it's your job to make them. And that's why it's so painful when you bomb; it's real-time feedback that you're failing.

But "the only failure is giving up" and "failure is only the opportunity to begin again, only this time more wisely" and "failure isn't failure if you finish your set and pretend you've learned something." So I pressed on and transitioned into my "Cliché" bit. I was already on stage, and they already didn't like me, so I might as well do what I came to do.

I finished my set and left the stage to an obligatory smattering of three collective claps from five people. The host hopped back up on stage and essentially ignored what just happened. "Alright, so we're going to take a fifteen-minute smoke break and come back with some more music."

I grabbed my bag and headed outside, ready for the day to be over. As I exited the bar, I passed one of the band members. He said, "That was pretty cool. I liked all of those sayings you put together."

"Thanks! You guys were great," I replied as I climbed over a mound of snow to get to my car.

If at least one person was listening, that counts as a show. My goal wasn't "have incredible sold-out performances in every state," though that would have been nice. My goal was simply to speak or perform in each one. And if it weren't for those five reactionless people, this trip to West Virginia would have been a waste.

But, regardless of how it went, it still got marked down in my spreadsheet. It was my own version of doesn't matter; had success. As Sheryl Sandberg says, "Done is better than perfect," and West Virginia was far from perfect, but at least it was done.

Tracking This Book

One of the best ways to stay focused on a task is to track it. That's why, over the years, I've collected data about nearly every aspect of my life, ranging from tracking how I spent my time for an entire year to every performance I've ever done. And because a book is essentially a collection of data, it can be tracked, analyzed, and processed, which is exactly what I've done. Here are some interesting stats about the collection of words you hold in your hands (or see on your screen):

- Number of Pages: **232**
- Number of Words: **78,114**
- Number of Unique Words: **8,486**
- Number of Characters (Literal): **422,495**
- Number of Characters (Figurative): **46**
- Number of Footnotes: **95**
- Number of URLs: **13***
- Number of References To: **Google (38), ghosts (31), donuts (21), milkshakes (16), waterfalls (7), hoodies (6), Adele (3), zombies (3), unicorns (2), Baberham Lincoln (1)**
- First Word (Alphabetically): **A**
- Last Word (Alphabetically): **Zoomed**
- First Word (Chronologically): **The**
- Last Word (Chronologically): **End**
- Most Frequently Used Word: **The**
- Most Frequently Used "Real" Word: **You**
- Number of Words Used 100 or More Times: **101**
- Number of Words Used Only Once: **4,321**
- Average Story Length (Words): **1,323**
- Shortest Story (Words): **New Mexico—922**
- Longest Story (Words): **California—1,772**

* See all of the links at trvn.us/50stateslinks.[88]

---

[88] Yes this link is included in the total above. Same thing for this footnote.

48. NORTH CAROLINA

What Do You Want to Do?
Durham, NC. January 28, 2016

I looked out at the eager faces of the students at Duke University. I was presenting to the Duke Association for Business Oriented Women, my fourth university program since arriving in the Raleigh/Durham area after my wonderful show in West Virginia three days prior. As I neared the conclusion of my program, I had opened things up for questions and was currently trying to decide how to best answer the query I was just presented.

After a moment of thought, I responded, "Let me answer your question with another question. How old do you think I am?"

The young woman who asked the question gave a quick pause before responding, "Thirty-two."

I was immediately offended. How dare she call me older than I really was? I wasn't thirty-two—yet. Not for at least another ten days.

"You're right," I said dejectedly. "I'll be thirty-two next month. I graduated from university back in 2006, which was—holy wow—that was ten years ago."

I hadn't really processed it until that moment. I graduated a decade ago. I realized that I was ancient in their eyes, an old man at an age they couldn't even fathom.

The same student raised her hand again. "Did you know that this was what you wanted to do when you graduated?"

It was a question I got a lot when people found out what I did for a living and one I had been thinking about that morning as I walked around the Coker Arboretum at the University of North Carolina. Being back on a college campus reminded me that I never imagined I'd have the life I had now back when I was still at school mostly because I didn't know this life existed.

"Not at all," I replied, happy to be talking about something other than how old I was to them. "I didn't know this was even a job when I graduated. I assumed I'd work in IT my entire career. I mean, my degree is in Computer Science and Engineering, and I sometimes think I understand computers more than I understand people.

"But to expand on your question, I think it's crazy for people to think you should have it all figured out by the time you graduate from college. I mean, imagine if we all stuck to the same fashion we had in school; I'd be in baggy clothes and a hoodie. Your parents would probably all be wearing spandex and big hair, and that's just your dads.

"And how boring would life be if you had everything figured out by the time you got your degree? There'd be no excitement, uncertainty, or intrigue. The truth is, you don't have to have it all figured out and, in fact, you can't. Because the world is constantly changing, and so are you. The Bureau of Labor and Statistics says the average person will have ten different jobs by the time they reach forty years of age. Ten! Because things change. Jobs change, and you change.

"Over time, you're going to learn what you like and don't like, what you want to do and what you want to avoid. The sad reality is that a lot of 'adults' forget: you are in control of what you do. If you end up in a job you hate, it's up to you to find ways to enjoy it or to find a new job. If you can't find a job, it's up to you to work on your networking and interviewing skills or to start your own business. Finding work that pays you enough and that you enjoy takes effort is not guaranteed or even owed to you. It's your responsibility."

I paused for a moment to let the message sink in and to think of what to say next. The students were leaning forward in their seats as a few scribbled notes on paper in front of them.

"No matter how good of a boss you have in the future or how great of a company you work for, no one will ever care more about your career than you. Well, except for maybe your mom."

A light chuckle spread across the room.

"So, you have to be proactive about what you want. Does that mean you have to have your life completely figured out by the age of twenty-two? Not at all, but you should have an idea of what you at least want to do next. Because what's the value of having a goal or a vision?"

The question was met with silence, possibly because they felt it was rhetorical.

"That's a real question: what's the value of having a vision?"

A woman from the back shared, "So you know where you're headed?"

"Absolutely," I said. "What else?"

"So you know what to do?" another student said.

"Yes! Having a vision of what you want long-term can help you make decisions. Have you guys heard of FOMO? The Fear of Missing Out? You see people doing these incredible things on social media, and you have this fear that you're missing out on something awesome. Having a vision mitigates FOMO. Because you can look at whatever that sexy new thing is and ask yourself, 'Will this get me closer to my goals?' If the answer is yes, do it. If it's no, you can comfortably say, 'That's cool, but it's not for me.'

"For example, I think being on *Saturday Night Live* would be pretty cool, right? And I have some friends who want to do that. I know some people who have done that. It would be cool, but it wouldn't help me become a better speaker. It wouldn't help me train organizations on how to use humor or teach individuals how to enjoy their jobs more. So it's not worth the incredible effort—and luck—that's required to get there. It's cool, but it's not for me.

"That said, if any of you know Lorne Michaels, feel free to make an introduction."

Another small laugh from the crowd. I started walking the room, making eye contact with students as I passed.

"So having some inkling of what you want long term can help you decide on what jobs to apply for or which job to take. But the other benefit of having a vision is that it can provide you with motivation. When you know your goal, and you know how your job is helping you reach that goal, it's much easier to do the work.

"I speak with a lot of companies who want to help their employees learn how to manage stress and prevent burnout, all while increasing employee engagement. One of the keys to doing that effectively is to help those employees realize why they are working at the company to begin with. Burnout doesn't happen from working too hard. Burnout happens from working really hard and not knowing what you're working for. Forty-plus hours a week at a job is only worth it . . . if it's actually worth it."

A hand slowly raised in the middle of the room. A quiet voice asked, "But what if we don't even know what we want long term? What if we don't have a vision?"

"That's awesome. That means you get to experiment. You get to try a bunch of things to see what you like, you get to have conversations with people to learn about what they do, and you get to ask yourself some powerful questions. It's good to know what you want to do, but more important than knowing is just wanting to know. To be curious about the question of what you want out of life.

"For many people, there are some common goals. Most people want financial security, a roof over their heads, and food on the table. They also want a job they enjoy, probably a significant other, and maybe kids one day. I want those things, plus I want to be able to travel and drink milkshakes. I want to feel like I'm having a positive impact on people's lives, and I want to make people laugh.

"Everything outside of that is just a detail. And figuring out those details is exciting because it means you get to try a bunch of stuff and see what sticks. Think you might want to be an accountant? Ask a few CPAs what their job is like and see if you would want to do that. Interested in politics? Shadow a local politician for a day. Want to be a comedian? Do an open mic and make people laugh. Your first job after school isn't for life; it's just for now. And when it no longer suits your needs, you can choose something else.

"And whenever you don't know what you want to do, try a bunch of things out. Before leaving P&G to start my own company, I tried a lot of different things to see what stuck. I did stand-up comedy on the road, I wrote for a sketch TV show, I helped write, produce, and edit a short film, and I spoke to different organizations. And the speaking, of everything I tried, stood out the most. It was the perfect intersection of making people laugh and getting to tell them what to do if they wanted to make a change. When I graduated, I had no idea that this was what I wanted to do, but I kept trying things on until I found something that fit."

I looked down at my watch. I was five minutes over my scheduled speaking time. I had gotten a little too excited to share my perspective with an audience at a crucial time in their lives. I walked back to the front of the room and looked back up at the students. "I am so sorry, I realized I've gone five minutes over. Why did no one tell me?"

A woman in the front responded, "Because we wanted to hear what you had to say. And it would have been awkward to mention something."

I apologized and gave a quick two-minute close to button everything up. The crowd applauded and started making their way out of the room. A line of students formed to talk with me and ask more questions. I smiled. Seeing as how I was the old, and maybe wise, man in the room to them, I was happy to provide as muchguidance as I could.

49. MARYLAND

Pics or It Didn't Happen
Baltimore, MD. February 1, 2016

If a tree falls in the forest, and no one is around to take a selfie with it, does it really matter? It's the philosophical question of our time. Selfies have become a part of mainstream culture, from Buzz Aldrin's selfie in outer space in 1966 to Ellen's selfie to break the internet in 2014. These self-indulgent photos give us a chance to show how cool we are. They aren't to say, "Look at the Grand Canyon!" They're for saying, "Look at *me* at the Grand Canyon."

Which is, admittedly, self-centered. I mean the word itself comes from the shortening of self-ego to self-E to selfie.[89]

So naturally, I decided to take a selfie in every state and compile them all into a video so everyone could see me see how cool the United States is.[90] Of course, that video is only complete if I have a selfie in every state. And if I forgot to take a selfie in a state I'd already been to, it meant I had to go back, which is why I found myself stepping off the Amtrak train at Pennsylvania Station in Baltimore, Maryland.

I was there for a singular purpose: to get a selfie. Yes, I completed North Carolina, returned the rental car to Georgia, flew from ATL to JFK, took a three-hour train ride from NYC, and would be taking another three-hour train ride back in a few hours, just to get a picture of myself, taken by myself.

---

89 Most people claim the term originated in Australia, where adding -ie to the ends of words is common slang, like *barbie, mozzie,* and *Aussie,* but who's to say we can't both be correct?
90 To see the video, visit tarv.in/50selfies

It wasn't necessarily what I wanted to do; it was what I had to do. Now, all I had to do was find the right background.

I exited the train station to find a light drizzle and a gray sky. The weather decided this trip wasn't going to be a pleasant experience. Based on what little I knew about Baltimore, that somehow seemed appropriate.

My only reference points for the city were that one of my exes was from there, it was home to my second least favorite NFL team (Steelers are the worst; Ravens are #2), and it was the setting for one of the best TV shows of all time, *The Wire*.

Given that I didn't want a picture of my ex's old house or M&T Bank Stadium, I elected to look for spots from *The Wire*. I stood under an overhang as I googled locations from the HBO show.

I had plenty of options. I could see the high-rises in West Baltimore or Bubbles' Garage in North Central. I could check out Hamsterdam in the East or McNulty's crash site in the Southeast. As the precipitation increased, I prioritized distance over beauty and settled on where some of the most important battles in the show happened: City Hall.

I made my way down toward my photospot as the drizzle continued to drop. The closer I got to the harbor, the more the wind whipped my face with a misty wetness. I took a left on East Lexington St. and walked a short distance before I saw the iconic-to-the-show building. It looked exactly as you would imagine a City Hall to look like: a rounded dome with a bell tower broke skywards from the rectangular structure below it. Windows wrapped the entire building in the impractical but aesthetically pleasing oval-at-top, rectangle-at-bottom shape, and flags flew anywhere you could stick a pole.

The rain started to let up as I tried to find the perfect angle that would get me and the hall in the background. I took out my phone and prepped for the picture.

A person's selfie process is like a fingerprint: unique to each individual and something that should be established at birth. Some people will always angle the camera from above, so they appear thinner. Others have a rare condition that whenever they see a reflection of their face in a phone, they automatically become a duck. Many people attempt to push the on-screen camera button; others have learned that, on most phones, the volume buttons will also snap a picture.

There are those who will take a selfie, study the results, and then take another picture, repeating twenty-seven times before ultimately deciding the first one was the best one. Others just take twenty-seven pictures in a row in quick succession assuming, by the law of averages, one will be good.

A few people like to amp themselves up for the photo. I once saw a guy in Norway taking selfies who would say "Cheese!" to himself, and just himself, before every picture he took. I was fully expecting him to say, "Great job, self. Now, as if you're a tiger, rawr!"

My process was simple. Phone goes in the right hand, arm fully extended. I frame the picture with my head at the top of the frame, background visible over my left shoulder. I occasionally smile but not often, instead electing for more of a slight smirk (this is true whether I'm at Disneyland or a cemetery). I take one picture, and then I move on. I don't look at the result until hours, days, or months later.

I lined up the shot up with City Hall in the background, *click*, and then I was done. A 400-mile round trip for a simple click of a button.

My mission was accomplished, but since I was there and the weather had gone from "ugh" to "meh," I decided to explore a little more of B-more. I walked down to the water, through a few small parks, and past a particularly cocky bench that claimed Baltimore as "The Greatest City in America." That's a bold claim for a city, where just a few streets away, was a strip club named the Jewel Box.

I also decided I should eat something local, so I did a quick search on what Baltimore was known for. Besides Edgar Allen Poe, The Inner Harbor, and crime, they were also renowned for the pit beef sandwich: tender rolls of beef piled high on a Kaiser roll with onions and tiger sauce.

I set out to find the local delicacy, though the path was not easy. The gods of food selection were tempting me that day as I had to pass a Shake Shack, home to my favorite burger on the planet, to find said sandwich.

I found a place called B&O American Brasserie and tried the Baltimore favorite. I had to admit: I was a fan. It was no Montana burrito or Oregon ice cream, but it was certainly better than anything they served at Primanti's in Pittsburgh.[91]

I headed back to the station and waited for my train. As I sat on an uncomfortable wooden bench facing the huge train schedule, I wondered if it was all worth it. Not just the trip to Maryland for a selfie, but the nomadic journey to all of the states. I was nearly complete with my goal of going to every state, and I wondered, what was it all for?

The deeper thoughts, the stories, and the lessons from each place would come later, but for that moment, I decided even if I learned nothing, of course it was all worth it.

Was my life significantly better now that I would have a picture of myself in all fifty states? Maybe not. But what else was I doing? If I had stayed in

---

91 Take that Pittsburgh; that'll show you for consistently knocking the Bengals out of the playoffs.

NYC that day, I would have spent my time sending emails and working on an upcoming presentation. Instead, I spent a collective six hours on a train, sending emails and working on an upcoming presentation.

The question wasn't necessarily why would I go all the way to Baltimore for a picture; the question was, why wouldn't I? I still got work done, and I went on a mini adventure in the process. Ignoring any value I gained from my jaunt down to Poe's hood, it gave me something to do, just as my nomadic journey had. It gave me a chance to travel, see new sights, meet new people, and eat new food.

So yes, it was worth it. It was all worth it, "The Greatest City in America" included. I nodded to myself, affirming my conclusion. I took out my phone and took a quick look to see how my selfie turned out. It wasn't the best picture I'd ever taken, but it inched me closer to my final destination.

50. HAWAII

The Story of a Story
Honolulu, HI. February 11, 2016

I stood at the top of Aloha Tower, looking out at the Pacific Ocean in front of me. My skin felt the warmth of the bright sun in the sky and the cool of a light breeze off the water. The scene was perfect.

That day, February 11, 2016, was a special day for me. First, I was in Honolulu, Hawaii. After taking a selfie in Maryland, returning to New York, and keynoting a conference in Alaska, I finally made it to my fiftieth state; my goal of seeing all of them was now complete.

That I should end on the fiftieth state admitted to the union, the one with beautiful beaches, incredible hikes, and an average temperature of seventy-eight degrees in February was no accident. Through some careful planning and a little luck, I was able to finish my quest in the last star of the flag. And that was important to me because I wanted the last state to be a highlight, not just an item on the checklist (sorry, North Dakota).[92]

Just traveling to the state and taking in its beauty would have been enough, but Hawaii offered me so much more. I stayed with a cousin whom I had never met who couldn't have been more welcoming. She took me to see whales and turtles off the coast and to the monument to honor those lost at Pearl Harbor. Her husband took me surfing for my very first time. I went

---

92 I don't mean this offensively; it's just that North Dakota realizes that, for some people, the only reason they visit the state is to complete all fifty. In fact, if you go to the visitor center and tell them it's your last state, they'll give you a T-shirt.

hiking on my own and jumped off rocks into a river. I visited the touristy beaches and drove nearly the entire island. I ate great food, met great people, and generally had a great time.

The second reason that day was special to me was that I was going to perform that night in a storytelling show. Circumstantially and through thoughtful planning, but not coincidentally, that show would be my 1,000th show as a performer.

Two months before, when I was closing in on a kilo of performances, I arranged my schedule such that my first show in quadruple digits would be in Hawaii. It just so happened that there was a storytelling show I could join whose theme matched perfectly with what I might want to talk about. The focus was "Should I stay or should I go? Stories about making big decisions and living with the consequences." Hmm, it seemed like I might have a story to tell.

The third reason for it being a special day was that it was also my 32nd birthday. I was entering my 11,669th day on the planet, 7,138 miles from where I was born, doing my 1,000th performance in my fiftieth state. It was going to be a great way to celebrate turning another year older.

As I do on every birthday, I wanted to take some time to reflect on the past year while drinking a milkshake. And that's how I had ended up at the top of Hello/Goodbye/Welcome/Love/Aloha Tower. I had picked up a milkshake from a nearby restaurant and was looking for a quiet place for contemplation when I found the spot with a majestic view.

As the sun and breeze continued their perfect harmony, I brought the chocolate shake to my lips and sucked on the straw. A lot had happened since my last b-day shake.

A year ago, I had one apartment, four rooms worth of stuff, and a handful of selfies. Now, I had zero apartments, two bags of stuff, and a selfie in every state. Indeed, a lot had changed.

I thought about the stories that had taken place during my last trip around the sun, not just for nostalgia but also because I still hadn't decided what I was going to say for the show that night. I thought about the "big stories," seeing the Grand Canyon in Arizona, pushing a Ferrari in California, and fending off a bear in Alaska. I reminisced about the "smaller ones," like hiking with Rachel in Connecticut, eating dinner with my mom in Ohio, and—seriously—I had to scare off a bear!

I grabbed my notebook from my bag and started working on an outline of what I wanted to say. I thought of the highs and lows, the funny situations and weird encounters, the comedic thoughts and poignant moments. And I thought about how I might share them with the audience that evening.

Stories are perhaps humanity's greatest communication device. After all, it's how we passed down information long before we had the internet, the printing press, or the written word. Stories have the ability to help us relive a moment, make it possible to learn from the experiences of others, and naturally hold our attention.

When we get together with old friends, we reminisce about the stories of our former selves. When we meet someone new, we tell the stories of who we are now. When we get pulled over by the cops, we come up with a story we hope justifies our speeding.

When people asked about my experiences as a nomad, they didn't care about the facts of my trip, though I had them readily available. They wanted to hear the stories of my travels, the ups and downs, the moments of interest. No one cares about the standard meal you ate at a fast food restaurant; they want to hear what a Chicken Fettuccine Alfredo Burrito tastes like. They don't care about the cookie-cutter hotel you stayed in; they want to learn what it's like to sleep in a car. They aren't interested in the regular open mics you did; they want to know about the time you tried to rap your way on to a hip-hop show.

Because, when a story is told right, the listener gets to live vicariously through the storyteller's experiences. They get to be entertained and engaged, and they learn the same lessons but without all the work. Because every story has a lesson, and every lesson has a story.

I thought about what lessons I learned from my journey, wondering how I might be different because of this adventure.

I was definitely more present. Not seeing people consistently meant that when I did see them, those moments were incredibly important. I was more conscious of not getting distracted by my phone or future plans while I was in the presence of someone else. Instead, I was working on staying in the now with that person.

I was also more aware of my prejudices and worked to manage my own preconceived notions about nouns: people, places, and things. The biker bar in South Dakota, the winery in Iowa, and the poetry show in Florida all gave me a new perspective on my own perspective.

And I was more grateful. I had the opportunity to see so many incredible places with so many awesome people while doing a job I absolutely loved. I was grateful for the support system that made it possible, the technology that made it easier, the people who made it worthwhile, and whatever combination of nature versus nurture versus decision-making versus luck that made the trip what it was.

I scribbled a few notes in my notebook to wrap up the story and finished off my milkshake. Over the next few hours, I would rehearse the story in my head, talk to family members as they wished me a happy birthday, and read hundreds of birthday wishes on Facebook. And that night, with a feeling of pride, a sense of accomplishment, and a bit of anxiety ("Will anyone care about this story?"), I performed in my 1,000th show, on my thirty-second birthday, in my fiftieth state.

The Story of My Year as a Nomad

This story was shared at the Civil Beat Storytelling Show *in Honolulu, HI on February 11, 2016.*[93]

Today, February 11, 2016, is a very special day for me. By speaking to all of you today, this marks my 1,000th show as a performer. I've also now spoken or performed in all fifty states. And today is my thirty-second birthday.

And in those thirty-two years, I've made a lot of big decisions—big ones like going to The Ohio State University and getting a degree in computer science and engineering. The decision to start an improv group while there. The decision to start working at Procter & Gamble after I graduated, the decision to move to New York City, the decision to leave Procter & Gamble to start my own company, teaching organizations how to use humor to be more productive.

And the decision I made on March 1, 2015, to become a nomad, to put all of my stuff in storage, aka my mom's place in Ohio, and live out of two carry-on bags, which I've been doing ever since.

The decision to be a nomad was surprisingly logical. If you know me, that's not all that surprising because I'm an engineer, so I'm driven more by logic than emotion. I make decisions not by feelings but by spreadsheets and flow-charts.

Becoming a nomad seemed logical. My lease was coming up in New York City, and I knew I was going to move, either to a borough or maybe to the West Coast. And I knew that for the six out of the next eight weeks, I was going to be traveling out of the country for work, and I wasn't going to be in any one spot. So I thought, well what if I just traveled indefinitely?

I knew there would be consequences of the decision; I knew it would be challenging, but I also knew I'd collect some pretty cool stories and some pretty cool experiences along the way.

What I didn't know was how it would change me. In some ways, small changes, like I'm definitely fatter. Not to say I'm fat, I'm just statistically fatter than I've ever been before. And I know that because I measure every single month.

---

93 To see the performance of this story, check out the video at tarv.in/nomadstory

Not because I'm obsessed with health, I just like to pretend to my life is a video game, and I want to have all the stats.

I've also changed in bigger ways, though. I've become more emotional, or at least aware of emotions. And that's big for me as an engineer. I feel like humans would be better served if they had error messages instead of emotions.

Instead of feeling overwhelmed and breaking down when things were tough, you'd just get a warning message that said, "Warning: System Overload. Please restart by taking a nap." And some error messages you wouldn't even have to change. Say you're out flirting with a waiter and she's not really feeling it, it'd just pop up "Error: Unable to establish connection to server." That would make things so much easier.

But being a nomad has changed how I think about emotions. Specifically one emotion in general, and that is gratitude. Because the thing about traveling to all of these different places is that I've met some phenomenal people. And I've had some incredible experiences, and I'm grateful for the people that I've met.

I'm grateful for the people in Pringle, South Dakota, population 112, who opened their doors to their music open mic and allowed me to perform at their biker bar doing some poetry to check off South Dakota as a state.

I'm grateful for the people I met randomly in the desert going from Las Vegas to Los Angeles, when a bunch of us, a caravan of random cars, saw traffic ahead so we all took a detour on Google Maps that took us down a dirt road. And six miles into the seven-mile dirt road, it went from dirt to sand, and we all got stuck.

And I remember we were pushing this car in front of us—it was an Enzo Ferrari—an Enzo Ferrari had taken this dirt road for some reason, and I'm pushing it alongside five other people from all of these different places, and the guy next to me says "Well, I didn't think I'd be doing this today." I said, "I don't think any of us expected to push a Ferrari in the desert today."

But I'm grateful for the people that I met as a result. I'm grateful for my second cousin, who's here tonight because she opened up her doors and allowed me to stay with her here in Hawaii, even though she had never met before. I'm grateful for those moments.

I'm also grateful for the moments that I've had with people that I care about. Because when you travel and you don't really see anyone regularly, the moments you do have with them become even more meaningful. Because as I've traveled, I've gone to some incredible places.

I've hiked the Grand Canyon, and it was gorgeous, but no hike compares to the one I went on with my brother, Dave, in Kasha Katuwe, New Mexico. Because as we hiked the very narrow canyon, it started to rain, and we hid under an overhang, and we let the rain fall down. And it reminded me of when we were kids growing up and we'd go on adventures in the very suburban Cincinnati, Ohio. We'd go out and explore and pretend like we were exploring a new world or that we were somehow transported to Jurassic Park. And that moment in Kasha Katuwe brought me back to the moment as kids. Things were pretty similar, although we were much older, we got tired a lot quicker, and it was like we exploring Jurassic World, not Jurassic Park.

I remembered being so grateful for the moment.

I was also grateful for all of the incredible sunsets I'd seen. I was at A La Moana Park yesterday, and I saw this gorgeous sunset, and it was absolutely pristine, but it didn't match the sunset that I had with my girlfriend Rachel, standing in the mud on the side of a non-descript hill in Palo Alto, California.

And I've had incredible moments like that, like going to an Ohio State game with my brother, Adam, or playing video games with my best friend, Nate. And it's those memories that I think I'm going to hang on to.

But most of all, I'll remember this park in Mason, Ohio, about five miles from where I grew up. The park itself isn't noteworthy at all. It's not on Lonely Planet's Top 10 Parks to Go To or anything; they don't even charge an admission to get in, but it's a special park to me because it's where me and my mom just walked and chatted, not about anything in particular. I couldn't even say what the subject was.

But I remember that moment walking around with my mom in this park, feeling so grateful for that opportunity. That's what I remember, and that's what changed for me as an engineer, feeling that emotion of gratitude.

I was in North Carolina a couple of weeks ago, it was my forty-ninth state, and I was talking with a friend of mine. We were having dinner, and she was like, "Wow, it sounds like you're living the life."

I don't know about that. I'm living *a* life; I don't know if it's *the* life. I don't have a house, I've worn the same four shirts for the past year (except for this one; it's new. I got it for Christmas). I don't carry more than three ounces of liquid on me at any time because of TSA. I don't think I'm living the life, but I am living my life, and I think that's what's been the impact.

I'm not entirely sure what's next. I know over the next two months I'm going to go to four or five countries for work. I'm going to multiple states. But I don't know where I'm going to end up after that. I do know that wherever I go, I'll be this more grateful person, this changed person. Because when you travel around and you don't really have a house anywhere, if you have friends and family and the kindness of strangers, you kind of have a home everywhere. And that's what I'm most grateful for. Thank you.

EPILOGUE

Brooklyn, NY. September 1, 2016

I took one last read-through and hit PUBLISH. My post, *18 Months as a Nomad—By the Numbers,* was now live on my site.[94] I leaned back in my chair and smiled. *My* chair, something I hadn't been able to say in a while. I was sitting at *my* desk, in *my* room, in *my* apartment. After 550 days, I was officially done with the nomadic journey.

Upon completing my goal of speaking or performing in all fifty states in February, I had continued to live as a nomad. I traveled to England, Scotland, Portugal, Spain, Singapore, and Malaysia. I returned to the Grand Canyon with my mom and brothers. Rachel and I made a road trip back east hitting gorgeous parks along the way. I spoke at some incredible conferences, did some hilarious shows, and ate a lot of delicious food.

I had completed my goal but continued to move. Part of it was logistical; I kept finding reasons for extended nonstop travel, either for work or holiday with friends and family.

A larger part of it was procrastinational; I couldn't decide where I wanted to live. Eventually, I narrowed it down to New York, San Francisco, or Los Angeles and created a spreadsheet weighing the pros and cons of all three. New York came out on top, beating San Francisco, 64 to 63.

The score was too close to make the decision easily, but then convenience stepped in. Three of my good friends in New York were in need of a room-

---

94 Check out the full stats from the post at tarv.in/nomadnumbers

mate. They had moved in together with a fourth friend who promptly got a writing job that took him to LA, and now they had a spare room in their four-bedroom place in Brooklyn.

I don't necessarily believe in fate, but I do believe in convenience. Moving in with Brady, Ian, and Matt was a no-brainer: I had stayed with them multiple times during my trips to New York, and we always got along well. Plus, if I moved in with them, I didn't have to worry about deciding on what neighborhood to live in, finding an apartment, paying a broker's fee, collecting ninety-two forms of ID, solving a Rubik's cube, destroying a Horcrux, and all the other things required to get an apartment in NYC.

And so, on September 1, 2016, the journey ended. And what a journey it had been. In total, I traveled an estimated 159,023 miles (that's 255,922 kilometers), or roughly six trips around the globe, equivalent to one circumnavigation every three months. And I did it all out of two carry-on bags.

I traveled to 142 different cities, all fifty states, fourteen countries, and three continents. I took sixty-six flights (not including layovers), 181 car trips, forty-seven trains (not including subways), eight buses, and one ferry. I did 151 engagements for work and 136 performances. I had an estimated one million milkshakes.

I took over 2,000 pictures, including a selfie in every state, countless pictures out the windows of airplanes, and a picture of a camel statue wearing a sombrero.

I saw old friends and new family and met new friends and old family. I chatted with strangers, performed for crowds where I knew no one, and saw a guitar-playing George RR Martin lookalike. And I found connection with the people of this country. Every state I went to, I felt welcomed and invited. And I know that's not true for everyone all of the time, but I realized that we're all just human, and when we remember that, when we remember we're all in this together, we treat each other a little better.

I also spent a ton of time alone. Eighty-eight percent of the miles I traveled were by myself. And in that time, I learned a lot about me. Oddly enough, as I became more comfortable with myself, I got more comfortable with other people. Meeting strangers for the first time used to be nerve-wracking; I was unsure of what to say and worried about what they thought of me. Now it was fun.

I could ask them about their experiences (conversation deferment), and I had some interesting stories to share if they asked me about mine. And I no longer obsessed about what they thought of me; there was already a small group of people in West Virginia that was unimpressed by my comedy and a woman in Pringle, South Dakota who was my biggest fan.

As an introvert, talking to new people will forever be draining to do, but I actually enjoyed it now. In large part, it was because I was now cool with this collection of cells I had become (and because I could tell people about this fun nomad adventure I did).

When I started my nomadic journey, I had no idea what to expect, how long it would last, or even why I was doing it. And you know that's true because that line, verbatim, is in the prologue. But after all was read and done, the journey surpassed any expectations I didn't know I had. Because technically, yes, I was the same human that left my NYC apartment eighteen months prior, but I was a different person. I was more self-aware, less self-absorbed, more confident, less shy, and more or less better all around. If this journey was an experiment in self-improvement, it passed with flying colors and was deserving of the blue ribbon at the science fair.

Sometimes the lessons I learned smacked me in the face (like when running through the park in Maine); more often they were more subtle (like when dealing with a talkative Uber driver in Washington). Personal growth wasn't always obvious. There wasn't always that flash-bang aha! moment where everything changes for you in a split second. Sometimes growth was a series of small changes and challenges that you don't even know are happening until, some time later when you realized you'd become someone different, someone better.

And along the way, through the personal change and self-reflection, the speaking engagements and performances, and the hundreds of thousands of miles traveled, I collected stories. Stories of the experience of a lifetime. Stories that told the beauty of this country, the kindness of its people, the deliciousness of its food, and the awfulness of the state of Michigan. Stories that I've already forgotten and stories that will stay with me for a lifetime. Stories of one comedian's journey through these *United States of Laughter*.

Fifty States, Fifty Lessons

My journey to all fifty states was a transformative experience, not just for me but also my shoes (they got pretty scuffed up). I'd venture to say that every state had some nugget of wisdom to be learned.

Granted, some of those learnings might be a tad forced, like trying to find meaning from the Beatles's "I Am the Walrus." But I've realized that's just called perspective. Yes, my experiences define me, but I also define my experience.[95] So here's what I learned from each state.

Alabama	Getting older doesn't mean you have to get old.
Alaska	Better to prepare and not need than to need what you didn't prepare.
Arizona	The best way to repay someone is to make their sacrifice worth it.
Arkansas	Don't forget your wallet; you tend to need money for things.
California	Hindsight is 20/20, foresight isn't guaranteed, so learn to take risks.
Colorado	Don't judge a park by its name.
Connecticut	Life isn't fair; it's also not unfair. It just is.
Delaware	Sometimes you have to risk your life to get a milkshake.
Florida	If you quit every time you failed, you would've never learned to walk.
Georgia	Incognito mode is your friend.
Hawaii	Every story has a lesson, and every lesson has a story.
Idaho	Preparation today means success tomorrow.
Illinois	Nothing in life is without consequence.
Indiana	Friends not only make happiness possible, they make it worthwhile.
Iowa	Don't judge a venue by its location behind a creepy house on a hill.
Kansas	You miss out on gas from 100% of the stations you don't stop at.
Kentucky	To find success you must first define success.
Louisiana	Do what makes you say, "Yeehaw."
Maine	Be efficient with tasks and effective with people.
Maryland	If you have the option for adventure, why not take it?
Massachusetts	Being right doesn't stop people from annoying the crap out of you.
Michigan	Travel changes your perspective, even when you don't want it to.
Minnesota	If you only focus on the ups and downs, you'll miss out on the middle.
Mississippi	Don't sleep in a car.
Missouri	True connection happens when the people behind the façades meet.
Montana	Diversity, collaboration, and gluttony make the US great.
Nebraska	I do not look like I can rap.

---

95 I am the walrus (goo goo g'joob).

Nevada	If you reflect too much on the past or focus too much on the future, you can easily miss the now.
New Hampshire	Your environment shapes your thoughts.
New Jersey	Don't let preconceptions prevent you from having a good time.
New Mexico	Don't relive your childhood; live your now-hood.
New York	Choose connection over competition.
North Carolina	Be curious about what you want out of life.
North Dakota	Every experience has a positive; sometimes it takes time to find it.
Ohio	The best place to return to is home.
Oklahoma	No matter the venue, the art still matters.
Oregon	Don't let one setback stop you from greatness.
Pennsylvania	The greatest payment for a job well done is appreciation (and money).
Rhode Island	Even introverts get lonely.
South Carolina	The road less traveled might be less traveled for a reason.
South Dakota	If it doesn't mean much for all of eternity, it better mean something for right now.
Tennessee	The world feels smaller when you stay connected.
Texas	Don't let choice become a chore.
Utah	Our only real constraints are the ones we give ourselves.
Vermont	Shut up to meet fascinating people.
Virginia	A tribe is a group that shares your sense of humor.
Washington	It's not always about what you want; it's about what others need.
West Virginia	Sometimes "meh" is the best you get.
Wisconsin	Fear is just an opportunity for planning.
Wyoming	Don't let past happiness be the cause of your current unhappiness.

ACKNOWLEDGMENTS

This wouldn't have been possible without the help and support of some incredible people. A huge thank you to:

Mom. For never-ending support throughout my travels and for always having a place to call home.

Adam. For always being willing to get Skyline with me and for teaching me the fun that an innocent prank can provide.

David. For all the adventures we were able to go on together and for driving during the days so I could get some work done (or secretly mess around on Reddit).

Rachel. For all the incredible support, patience, and understanding. And for the sash when I completed my fiftieth state.

Nate. For keeping me sane and level-headed through everything and always being just a phone call away.

Raman. For being a strong advocate for me even trying to live as a nomad and giving me competition for seeing all fifty states.

Christopher. For helping me understand what these stories might mean to myself and others, and for always having Gatorade for me when we met.

Brady, Ian, and Matt. For giving me a place to stay whenever I was in New York and for being my new place of residence when I finished my journey.

The Taylor and Boland Families. For giving me a place to stay in in San Francisco and Honolulu, for helping me find new adventures, and for supporting me at my shows.

Everyone in the CSz family. For opening their arms, homes, and stages for me whenever I was in one of their cities.

To Jaclynn for the Detroit tour, Michelle for the speaker coaching, Tamara for exchanging travel stories, the Ramirez/Roy family for letting me shoot guns, and to Rachel G, the Starrs, Kevin, Joe, Sarah, Bobbi, Lauren, Dan, Debra, Courtney, Tammy, Pat, Colby, Tim, Chris, Chris, and everyone who let me crash on their couch or sleep in their guest room. To Ann for help in organizing this written experience, and Phil and the entire team at Red Brush for helping get it out to the world. To the Pomodoro Technique, without which this book would have never been completed.

THE END OF THE ROAD

Really? After more than 77,000 words you're still here? Normally this is where the "About the Author" section would go, but my guess is that you probably have a good sense of who I am by now.

If you still want more, feel free to continue the conversation:

Instagram: @drewtarvin
Twitter: @drewtarvin
Flickr: flickr.com/drewtarvin
Facebook: facebook.com/drewtarvin
LinkedIn: linkedin.com/in/andrewtarvin

Find more details about this book at: drewtarvin.com
Find more about my speaking at: andrewtarvin.com
Find more about humor at: humorthatworks.com

OK, that's seriously enough. The End.

78857082R00144